The
MIRACLE
of a
DEFINITE
CHIEF
AIM

The Napoleon Hill Success Course series™

The Miracle of a Definite Chief Aim
The Power of the Master Mind
Thrive Through Organized Thinking
Autosuggestion: Your Key to a New Life
Secrets of Self-Mastery
Profiting from Failure
Winning Through Charisma
The Magic of Enthusiasm
The Sixth Sense: Your Connection to the Infinite
The Golden Rule: Your Inner Secret to Prosperity & Power

The Napoleon Hill Success Course series™

The MIRACLE of a DEFINITE CHIEF AIM

MITCH HOROWITZ

Inspired by the Teachings of

NAPOLEON HILL

An Approved Publication of the Napoleon Hill Foundation

Published by Gildan Media LLC
aka G&D Media
www.GandDmedia.com

Copyright © 2017 The Napoleon Hill Foundation
Portrait of Napoleon Hill copyright © 2017 by Tim Botta

First Trade Paperback Edition: 2018

Front Cover design by David Rheinhardt of Pyrographx

Interior design by Meghan Day Healey of Story Horse, LLC.

Library of Congress Cataloging-in-Publication Data
is available upon request

ISBN: 978-1-7225-1005-3

Manufactured in the United States of America
by LSC Communications

10 9 8 7 6 5 4 3 2 1

To the members of my Master Mind group.

"Intolerance closes the book of knowledge and writes on the cover, 'Finis! I have learned it all!'

Intolerance makes enemies of those who should be friends. It destroys opportunity and fills the mind with doubt, mistrust, and prejudice."

— Napoleon Hill, "The Law of Success"

PORTRAIT OF NAPOLEON HILL BY TIM BOTTA

Contents

Introduction

The Power of a Single Focus

"Man's clarified desires are seeds containing
the power and plans of self-expression."
—Neville Goddard

I have spent more than twenty years as an author, publisher, and personal seeker in the world of positive-mind metaphysics and motivational philosophy. Experience has taught me this: No single factor under human control is of greater consequence than *one passionately felt and clearly formed aim.* And no modern writer has been more persuasive on this point than Napoleon Hill.

As Hill described it, beginning in 1908, at the urging of industrialist Andrew Carnegie, he began an intensive study of the traits that produce personal greatness in any field, from finance and science to art and politics. He codified these traits into his 1937 classic *Think and Grow Rich,* as well as in many other books, articles, and lectures. Although Hill identified (depending on the book) sixteen habits of high achievers, he emphasized one principle above all others: The necessity of a *Definite Chief Aim.*

Hill placed so much stock in this one core principle that he often capitalized Definite Chief Aim, which I refer to in this book as your **DCA**.

A definite aim is not a vague wish or desire to "be rich" or to "be successful." These kinds of random thoughts, Hill taught, often lead to apathy, unfulfilled dreams, and failure.

Rather, an authentic Definite Chief Aim means a specific, concrete goal on which, outside of the requisites of health and family, you base your entire existence. Although your DCA can, and should, be bold and even audacious, it must also be *reasonable*. Hill did not believe in chimeras or undirected daydreams. He believed in action. And effective action can be undertaken only by people who possess, or are ready to acquire, the training needed for scaling life's heights. The starting point of all action, and of all greatness, Hill insisted, is this one passionately felt and cherished aim. It is the closest thing life grants us to a magic formula.

Does that claim sound fanciful to you? Do you doubt that a clear, focused aim can radically change your life? Let me tell you a short personal story—you'll hear many others in this book, but this one is my own.

Like Hill, I began my career as a journalist. But I was unhappy. I didn't want to write about other people's trials and accomplishments. I wanted to forge my own, and in my own way. Leaving journalism, I felt directionless. I sought and attained a successful career in publishing. For a decade or so I thrived in the field—but something was missing. I didn't feel that I squarely *stood* for anything. I was still working on other people's dreams. As the new millennium dawned, and I entered my mid-thirties, I found that I missed writing—but that seemed like a path long left behind.

In the summer of 2003, a few months before my 38th birthday, a special opportunity arrived. The editors of *Science of Mind* magazine—a positive-thinking monthly founded in 1927 by minister and writer Ernest Holmes—asked me to interview All-Star pitcher Barry Zito. Barry made positive-mind metaphysics a central part of his training program. Interviewing him and writing the piece, "Barry's Way," helped me rediscover my passion and direction as a writer. I didn't fully know it at the time but I had found my DCA: To be a historian of alternative spirituality and self-help movements. (I am also, as you'll see from this book, a "believing historian.") Although I might not have gotten the message then, Barry's father, Joe Zito, apparently did. Two weeks after the article appeared, Joe, who I had never met, called me and, in his drill-sergeant voice, commanded: "Mitch, you stick with this thing!" Within three years—coinciding with the birth of our second son—I had my first book contract with Random House. Much else followed.

People asked how I could possibly find time to write as a father, husband, and publishing executive at Penguin. (Being a writer doesn't mean quitting your day job.) All I could reply was: "I want to write more than I want to sleep." That remains true today. And that's the hallmark of a Definite Chief Aim: something that is clear, action-oriented, doable, and evokes uncompromising passion.

I firmly believe that if you really want to find your aim in life, this book, and others in the Napoleon Hill Success Course series, will lead you to identify and act on it.

The Miracle of a Definite Chief Aim is my first of ten volumes that take a deep dive into Hill's ideas. All of these books help you better apply Hill's principles, in whatever circumstances you find yourself. This book is based closely and faithfully on the principles, terms, and concepts of Napoleon Hill. Most of the book's anecdotes, reportage, and exercises are my own, and, as you will see, many sections (particularly those dealing with the arts and sciences) are contemporary. But all are inspired by the work of Napoleon Hill. In certain cases I emphasize an idea of Hill's that is especially relevant to 21st century readers, such as starting over after setbacks, or altering a Definite Chief Aim if conditions demand it. Each chapter contains one or more boxed "Action Steps"—additional exercises that work out your mental and emotional muscles, and give you fuller use of the ideas we explore. You can return to the Action Steps, as well as the Takeaway Points at the end of each chapter, as refreshers.

I pledge this to you: I do not sell fantasies or propagate ideas that I have not personally and effectively used myself. Neither did Napoleon Hill. This book is for practical dreamers—and actual doers. It is not for people who fantasize while drifting to sleep at night in front of a flickering television with a bag of chips lying on their chest. It is for people who hunger, above all else, to pursue their business, art, profession, invention, or special calling in life. Those are the people who almost always succeed, one way or another.

A miracle, in the classical sense, is a bending of natural laws by Divine intercession. For our purposes here, I define a miracle as a favorable deviation from all reasonable expectancy, such as the realization of a cherished but remote goal. This kind of a miracle, which is very possible, begins with the formulation of one clear, passionately felt aim, backed with intelligent action.

Let me put it another way. I once described *Think and Grow Rich* in a single sentence: "Emotionalized thought directed toward one passionately held aim—aided by organized planning and the Master Mind—is the root of all accomplishment." (If any of my terms are unfamiliar jump ahead to the appendix where I define Hill's "Sixteen Laws of Success.")

A definite aim is the foundation of any form of achievement. I have experienced this in my own life and witnessed it in the lives of others I know and admire, some of whom you will meet in the pages ahead. I have also watched capable people indecisively stumble from mediocrity to mediocrity—until the importance of having a DCA seeped in, and changed everything. In writing this book, it is my fondest hope that you witness the power of a definite aim in your own experience.

The Miracle of a Definite Chief Aim shows you, step by step, how to understand and apply Hill's principle, whatever your goal or values. Without a firm grasp of this idea, none of Hill's other lessons (or any motivational lessons for that matter) will work for you. As you will discover, having a definite chief aim will serve you whether you want to make money, express yourself in the arts, become a leader in your field, or defeat injustice and evil. Some of us want all these things. But the door of greatness cracks open only to those who approach their dreams with one special, overarching focus—a Definite Chief Aim. Let's find your aim together.

1

The Miracle of
Your Definite Chief Aim

What do you want out of life?

Be very careful how you respond to that question. It will make the difference between success and failure. Those who answer in a hasty or lazy way, or with bland generalities—like "I want lots of money"—are destined to go nowhere. The same is true of those who reply in a scattershot way, naming a plethora of wants and desires, many of which are self-contradictory, such as being a great leader and also having lots of leisure time, or traveling to exotic locales while also raising a young family.

But the person who can respond to the question of what he wants from life with one clear, definite, and *passionately* felt aim—that individual is going to succeed.

Did you notice the emphasis I gave to the word *passionately*? Your aim must be not only focused and specific—it must be so deeply held that, next to health and home, you desire it more than anything else. It must be something that you are willing to stake your life on. I don't mean that in a figurative or colorful way. I mean it with complete seriousness. Your Definite Chief Aim, or DCA, must be more than a mere want or desire, something that is likely to change as circumstances change. No. It must be an obsession: overwhelming, persistent, and single-minded.

The Power of a Single Wish

Does this criterion sound extreme? It is not. Let me tell you a story about someone you may have heard of: Bill Wilson. Bill went from being a street drunk to founding the worldwide fellowship Alcoholics Anonymous. He was one of the originators of the twelve-step method of recovery, which has rescued millions of people from addictions ranging from substance abuse to compulsive gambling to chronic debt spending. By the time of Bill's death in 1971, he was loved and admired by people around the world.

But in the early 1930s, when Bill was nearing forty, he was a wasted, rundown, and destitute drunk. His alcohol abuse had grown so unremitting that his existence became little more than a cycle of on-and-off stays in New York hospitals to dry out, while his wife, Lois, held down odd jobs to keep the couple clothed and fed. Bill was a failure in every sense. He was headed for a life of indigence and early death, either from an alcohol-related disease or a fatal accident while drunk.

Hitting bottom helped Bill formulate his Definite Chief Aim. It was to stay sober and help others to do the same. These were not two separate goals. Bill discovered that remaining sober and helping others to do so are one and the same. He built Alcoholics Anonymous on the principle of mutual service. Counseling and lifting up another addict are central to one's own recovery.

Bill arrived at his earliest insights for overcoming addiction during what he described as a spiritual awakening in December 1934. At the time, Bill was laid up in Towns Hospital in Manhattan, a place where he frequently retreated to recover from benders. "Lying there in conflict," Bill wrote, "I dropped into the blackest depression I had ever known. Momentarily my prideful obstinacy was crushed. I cried out, 'Now I'm ready to do anything . . .'"

What happened next upended his life: Bill said he had an experience of total freedom, euphoria, and absolute focus. "Blazing, there came the tremendous thought 'You are a free man.'" Bill felt that a Higher Power, as he phrased it, could help him and others recover from the crippling need to drink. In the years immediately following, Bill codified his experience into the twelve steps of Alcoholics Anonymous, and wrote a book of the same name.

But there is more to Bill's story. One of his closest collaborators and sources of inspiration in the 1930s was an old friend and ex-drinking buddy named Ebby Thatcher. But Ebby, the man who inspired Bill's interest in spiritual self-help, soon relapsed into drunkenness. Ebby spent much of his life struggling with alcohol, often ill and destitute. When he died in 1966, Ebby was sober but living as a dependent at a recovery center in upstate New York. Bill regularly sent him checks to keep him going.

Why did one man remain sober and another fall down? The difference pivots on Bill's Definite Chief Aim. Lois Wilson, Bill's wife, explained, in her typically understated manner, the difference she saw between the two men. In so doing, Lois illuminated the power behind having a single, paramount aim:

> After those first two years . . . why did Ebby get drunk? It was he who gave Bill the philosophy that kept him sober. Why didn't it keep Ebby sober? He was sincere, I'm sure. Perhaps it was a difference in the degree of wanting sobriety. Bill wanted it with his whole soul. Ebby may have wanted it simply to keep out of trouble.

Bill wanted it with his whole soul. Remember that sentence. It contains an extraordinary truth. Within the parameters of physical possibility, you receive what you "want with your whole soul"—whether inner truth, career success, riches, relationships, whatever it is. Excluding some great countervailing force—and for either good or ill—the single thing that you want above all else is *what you get.* That is the bargain life gives us.

Transcendentalist philosopher Ralph Waldo Emerson wrote that the key to power and achievement is found in "concentration"—he did not mean mental concentration, although that is an obvious virtue; but rather the philosopher meant focusing all of your thoughts and efforts on one specific, well-defined aim. Here is how Emerson put it in his essay *Powers and Laws of Thought.* I recommend that you write down this passage, place it somewhere you can regularly see it, and refer back to it frequently:

> The secret of power, intellectual or physical, is concentration, and all concentration involves of necessity a certain narrowness. It is a law of Nature that he who looks at one thing must turn his eyes from every other thing in the universe. The horse goes better with blinders, and the man for dedication to his task. If you ask what compensation is made for inevitable narrowness, why, this, that in learning one thing you will learn all things.

People make excuses why they cannot act on the one thing that they long to do. They say they cannot possibly make a living at it, or they don't know where to begin. Money concerns are important—and we deal with them in the chapters ahead, particularly chapter four. But the foregoing statements are often alibis for inertia. You can always *begin* something.

In 1964, the spiritual teacher Jiddu Krishnamurti conducted a series of dialogues with young students in India. The teacher spoke of the dulling effect of conformity, and the need to live by your own inner light. A boy asked him: "How can we put into practice what you are telling us?" Krishnamurti replied that if we want something badly enough, we know exactly what to do. "When you meet a cobra on the road," the teacher said, "you don't ask 'What am I do to?' You understand very well the danger of a cobra and you stay away from it." Krishnamurti noted:

You hear something which you think is right and you want to carry it out in your everyday life; so there is a gap between what you think and what you do, is there not? You think one thing, and you are doing something else. But you want to put into practice what you think, so there is this gap between action and thought; and then you ask how to bridge the gap, how to link your thinking to your action.

Now, when you want to do something very much, you do it, don't you? When you want to go and play cricket, or do some other thing in which you are really interested, you find ways and means of doing it; you never ask how to put it into practice. You do it because you are eager, because your whole being, your mind and heart are in it.

We have no claim on any aim save the one that we want with everything in us. But what if someone doesn't possess a single soul truth? This may be the meaning behind *Revelation* 3:16, which condemns those who are *lukewarm*: "So then because thou art lukewarm, and neither cold nor hot, I will spit thee out of my mouth." The hesitators, the undecided, those who commit to no path—they receive nothing. Life permits no halfway measures.

In that sense, the search for a DCA places a demand on you, one that you may think you've risen to but have never really tried. It is simply: *To come to terms with precisely what you want.* But within this simple instruction lies a danger. We are conditioned by habit and culture to think that we already know what we want, without really examining our assumptions. Yet when you organize your thoughts in a certain way—with a fearless maturity and honesty—you may be surprised to discover what your desires really are. A person who thinks of himself as "spiritual" may uncover a deep wish for worldly attainment; someone who has labored to support the work of others, or of family members, may find that she has her own deeply unsettled yearnings for self-expression; a person who is very public and extroverted may discover that he really wants solitude.

Does any of this mean that you, like Bill, must have a "spiritual experience" in order to arrive at your DCA? No, it does not. I don't care whether you're a believer, an agnostic, or an atheist. I am not here to sell you on religion (though I happen to believe that contemplative religion is the greatest force for good the world has ever known). I am here strictly to sell you on your own self-potential. What you need is an experience of absolute clarity—call it an epiphany, if you like—where you come to realize the nature of your truest aims. The capitalist philosopher Ayn Rand was a resolute atheist. But Rand, rejecting all theistic language and ideas, insisted that a person must reach a point of absolute self-clarity in which he knows, rationally and without any question, his true purpose in life.

Once that purpose, you can also call it your Higher Purpose, is realized, the energies of your existence begin to organize around it. Time becomes more productive. Relationships become richer (because you treasure contacts that are authentic and productive, and discard those that merely mark off time). Your moods improve. Your intellectual powers broaden and quicken. You detect connections among people and topics where you hadn't previously seen any. It takes a great deal of work and self-scrutiny to reach this stage of purposeful self-awareness. It is worth it. This book is focused on methods that will get you there.

The Power of a *Positive* Obsession

Do you want to make lots of money? Most of you coming to this book probably do. That is a fine and noble aim. You can do far more good with money than without it. You can help people you love. You can support schools, philanthropies, hospitals, houses of worship, and foreign-aid organizations. You can rescue people in trouble. You can also experience some of the finer things in life, such as travel, culture, and beauty. These are all sound pursuits. But "earning lots of money" is, in itself, insufficient as a DCA. The desire to "get rich" will not win you riches.

Here is a great and valuable secret, and I want you to pay close attention to it: *Your aim must provide a definite and self-evident service to the world.* You must then execute this aim with persistence, determination, and organized planning. Do this, and you will likely become rich. Or, depending on the nature of your desire, perhaps you will not become rich, but you will be fulfilled and useful—and be at least materially comfortable. Above all, *you must not be general.* Generality fritters away your energies. You must have a specific and constructive goal that dominates your hands, heart, and intellect, and fills a human need. (We will explore this last point in detail in chapter three, *But Is It Good?*)

Napoleon Hill went as far to say that your aim must assume the form of an obsession. In today's terms we think of an obsession as a harmful distraction, something that negates healthy pursuits in life and must be treated like a symptom and relieved. But the fact is, if you look at the lives of exceptional figures, whether artists, scientists, or business people, their achievements often grew out of one all-consuming, obsessive desire. It is not just any desire, but one that can be translated into its physical equivalent and that provides a constructive end product.

Hill often reflected on the case of Gilded Age steel magnate Andrew Carnegie. Carnegie told Hill in an interview that the most important principle of achievement on which he forged his career was singularity of purpose. Hill paraphrased him:

> Study any person who is known to be a permanent success and you will find that he has a Definite Major Goal; he has a plan for the attainment of this goal; he devotes the major portion of his thoughts and his efforts to the attainment of this purpose. My own major purpose is that of making and marketing steel. I conceived that purpose while working as a laborer. It became an obsession with me. I took it to bed with me at night, and I took it to work with me in the morning. My Definite Purpose became more than a mere wish; it became my Burning Desire! That is the only sort of definite purpose that seems to

bring desired results. Emphasize, through every means at your command, the vast difference between a mere wish and a burning desire that has assumed the proportions of an obsession. Everyone wishes for the better things of life, such as money, a good position, fame, and recognition; but most people never go far beyond the "wishing" stage. Men who know exactly what they want of life, and are determined to get it, do not stop with wishing. They intensify their wishes into a burning desire, and back that desire with continuous effort based on a sound plan.

Now, the desire to make steel may not sound terribly romantic to you. Maybe you want to correct injustice in the world; cure a disease; become a Wall Street wizard; or pursue a career in teaching or the arts. No matter. What Carnegie is saying provides the necessary mindset for all achievement. Again it must be stressed: *the only person who gets anywhere in his or her chosen field is the one who pursues it as a matter of passion and obsession.* This is also why you must select a DCA that inspires you with love, yearning, and drive; your aim must have *powerful emotions* at the back of it.

Rolling Stones guitarist Keith Richards said that he realized his life's aim when, as a budding musician in the mid-1950s, he heard the playing style of Elvis Presley's first guitarist, Scotty Moore. "All I wanted to do in the world was to be able to play and sound like that," Richards said. "Everyone else wanted to be Elvis. I wanted to be Scotty." That is what a passionate aim sounds like: It must be simple in conception, emotional to the core, and, like any worthy aim, requires immense work, training, and sweat equity, as well as a natural proclivity, topics to which we will return.

The Magic of Focus

Joseph Murphy was one of the greatest writers of popular metaphysics of the past century. A native of Ireland, Murphy relocated to New York in the early 1930s to seek a career as a chemist. Although he had a background in the sciences, the immigrant took a deep interest in the "new metaphysics" then sweeping the Western world. Murphy was fascinated with the philosophies of New Thought, Christian Science, and the "power of positive thinking"—all of which teach, in varying ways, that there exists a Divine Intelligence in the universe, and the developed person can use this power, or rather be used by it, through the medium of his thoughts.

After working as a druggist at a pharmacy counter at New York's Algonquin Hotel, Murphy came to realize that he possessed a talent for cogently and persuasively communicating spiritual and mental formulas, which he believed could produce success in the individual, in the same way that a chemical compound could produce a repeatable physical reaction. Murphy came to see the subconscious mind as a kind of homing device, and once impressed with an idea or conviction, the subconscious finds ways and means, sometimes beyond all expectation, to bring that concept into action.

Murphy soon left his career as a chemist to become a writer and metaphysical minister. In his most influential book, *The Power of Your Subconscious Mind*, published in 1963, he described three steps to success: 1) loving your work; 2) specializing within your field; and 3) providing service through your work. We will briefly examine each of Murphy's principles, and how they lead to your DCA.

The *first step*, Murphy wrote, is to discover the thing that you love to do and find some way, however rudimentary and nascent, of putting it into action. The greatest guarantee of success, he taught, comes from loving your work. If you love what you do you not only gain intrinsic pleasure from it, at least most of the time, but your enthusiasm bolsters the quality of your output and, hence, your capacity for success.

Some people complain that they have no sense of what they would love to do. I hear this problem often, and we will revisit it at several points. In such a case, Murphy advised meditating on the following passage: *The Infinite Intelligence of my subconscious mind reveals to me my true place in life.* Repeat this mediation to yourself quietly, positively, and lovingly to impress it upon your subconscious mind.

Two ingredients are vital in the effective use of meditations or affirmations: 1) feeling and 2) timing. Meditations must not be idle repetitions. The words themselves have no magic. To summon your creative energies you must say the words with deep and sincere emotional conviction. Do not force yourself. If you are not "in the mood" then return to the practice when you are. We all experience the coming and going of emotional states, like the ebb and flow of tides. Use these emotional states: When you are at ease, confident, rested, and hopefully expectant—that is the prime moment to work with your meditations. Be persistent and steady in your practice.

Regarding timing, it is best to whisper meditations to yourself in the moments just before falling asleep at night and just upon waking in the morning. This period of time, during which you hover been a state of sleep and wakefulness (and during which your body is exquisitely relaxed), is sometimes called the hypnagogic state. It is a time in which your subconscious mind is most impressionable, a topic to which we will return.

As you persist in this with ease and confidence, the nature of your aim, and of the work you most love, may arrive as a feeling, a hunch, or a tendency in a certain direction. It will probably come to you clearly and with a gentle surge of enthusiasm and inner awareness.

Murphy's *second step* to devising a promising aim is to *specialize* in some particular branch of work—and to strive to know more about it than anyone else. For example, Murphy said, if a student chooses chemistry as his profession, he should concentrate on one of the many branches or sub-branches of the field. He should give all of his time and attention to his chosen specialty. He should become sufficiently enthusiastic to know all there is about it and all the developments in the field. Being a generalist is overrated. Specificity and depth are what gives rise to greatness. No surgeon describes himself in general terms—each specializes in a particular organ or operation. This is the formula for distinction in every field: Let your knowledge run narrow and deep.

The *third step* is the one that Murphy considered the most important. You must be certain that the thing you want to do does not build your success only. *Your desire must not be characterized by mere money-getting or greed; it must benefit other individuals.* The path of a complete circuit must be formed. Every transaction must help fulfill the needs of others, as well as your own. If it is to benefit you alone, the circle or circuit is not formed, and happiness, productivity, and usefulness will not be lasting. In a key passage from *Think and Grow Rich*, Napoleon Hill prescribed repeating the following statement at least once daily:

> I fully realize that no wealth or position can long endure unless built upon truth and justice. Therefore, I will engage in no transaction that does not benefit all whom it affects. I will succeed by attracting to myself the forces I wish to use, and the cooperation of other people. I will induce others to serve me, because of my willingness to serve others. I will eliminate hatred, envy, jealousy, selfishness, and cynicism, by developing love for all humanity, because I know that a negative attitude toward others can never bring me success. I will cause others to believe in me because I will believe in them, and in myself.

This pledge does a good job of capturing what Murphy was after. Hang it above your desk or tape it to your desktop computer. As will be explored, our thoughts not only about ourselves *but also about others* have the same effect in our lives: What you believe—whether about yourself or a colleague—distinctly colors your day-to-day experience. There is greater truth in this than may first appear. We will revisit this point in chapter three.

In sum: The combination of 1) love for a project; 2) specialization and determination to know all there is about it; and 3) certainty that your project or transaction is of clear benefit to others, not just to you alone, forms an incredibly effective triad of focus. This kind of focus keeps you on track, sets you up to meet people and encounter opportunities that are pertinent to your aim, gives you and those around you the confidence that you are rightly progressing in your work, and, most importantly, places emotion at the back of your desire. Murphy's formula is, in essence, a three-step process to devising and beginning your Definite Chief Aim.

Directed Mental Force

The way that you think about your goal, and yourself, makes a concrete difference. Contemporary neuroscience has validated the point of view that persistent thoughts, backed by emotion, possess a special power. This is seen in the field of brain science called neuroplasticity, which has gained prominence in the early twenty-first century. In short, researchers at UCLA and elsewhere have discovered that people suffering from obsessive-compulsive disorder (OCD) can literally alter their neural pathways through a sustained program of redirected thought. Brain scans show that the nature of your thoughts can actually "rewire" your brain biology.

One of the most active and practical experimenters in neuroplasticity is research psychiatrist Jeffrey M. Schwartz. Schwartz has designed a program that teaches people with OCD to divert their thoughts away from intrusive or ritualistic impulses. His regimen—and this is vital to our concern here—specifies that *the redirected, healthy thought must be focused on something that is enjoyable, whether music, physical activity, eating,* and so on. You are not built to control your mind through an act of will alone. Trying to control your thoughts or emotions is often frustratingly evasive and depleting. But you *are built to gravitate toward passionately felt desires,* which is the lynchpin to Schwartz's treatment. Again, the subject must redirect his thoughts away from obsessive or ritualistic drives toward something that is pleasurable. This "directed mental force" eventually results in a rewiring of the brain's neural pathways, through which electrical impulses travel.

Neuroplasticity underscores why you must select a DCA that taps into your deepest yearnings. Doing so is a form of insurance against distraction, wandering thoughts, apathy, and—the all-time progress killer—procrastination. "Do what you love" is not just some pretty slogan. It is the very thing that will get you *working,* and deliver you from mental diversions. This is true in more than just a figurative way. "I propose," Schwartz says, "that the time has come for science to confront serious implications of the fact that directed, willed mental activity can clearly and systematically alter brain function; that the exertion of willful effort generates a *physical force* that has the power to change how the brain works and even its physical structure."

Stronger Every Day

Another reason why a passionately felt DCA gets you where you're going is that it sets in motion the principle of *autosuggestion*. Autosuggestion is a term coined in the early twentieth century by French hypnotherapist Emile Coué. You may know of Coué's confidence-building mantra: "Day by day, in every way, I am getting better and better." The mind-pioneer recommended gently repeating the formula twenty times just before drifting to sleep at night and twenty times upon awakening in the morning.

During these "in between" states you are conscious of sensory information. Your mind is flooded with stream-of-consciousness ideas and mental pictures. But your rational defenses are down. Your logical functioning is at low point. This is why people who are grieving or suffering from depression often describe the dawning hours of the morning as the most painful time of day. These periods are most definitely not the time to problem-solve or think about challenges. Our capacites for perspective and proportion are at their weakest, and the gremlins of our subconscious and our emotions are in the driver's seat, so to speak.

There is, however, a way to make this hypnagogic state work for your aims. Because your rational defenses are lowered, it is an excellent time to impress ideas on your psyche through meditations and affirmations, like those of Joseph Murphy and Emile Coué. One of the biggest problems with repeating affirmations is that the logical mind may reject them: If you don't *feel* prosperous, well, or strong, for example, your rational mind may mount a resistance that leaves you feeling worse than before. But when the gates of rationality are down, Coué and others have theorized that affirmations can more easily penetrate the subconscious and form emotional memories, in the same way that you vividly recall, and sometimes relive, childhood episodes, both happy and sad.

Researchers at Cambridge University and elsewhere are paying new attention to the hypnagogic state, trying to gain a better understanding how our minds function during these fragmentary periods when perceptions are more easily accepted and our sense of reality is pliable. Hypnagogia is one of several areas where French mind pioneer Coué demonstrated early insights, which twenty-first century researchers are now validating.

Placebo researchers at Harvard Medical School recently, though inadvertently, followed one of Coué's threads. In January 2014, a medical school study reported that migraine sufferers responded better to medication when given "positive information" about a drug. Coué made that exact observation in the early 1900s while working as a pharmacist in northwestern France. He found that patients benefited more fully from medication when he spoke in praise of a formula. This insight led to his "day by day" affirmation. Coué believed that anyone, with almost any need, could stimulate the same positive mental forces he encouraged among patients by routinely whispering the famous mantra.

The Harvard researchers, while echoing Coué's century-old insight, arrived independently at their conclusions. Their paper made no mention of the therapist.

But Coue's work was known to one of the study's architects, Ted Kaptchuk, who directs Harvard's program in placebo research. "Of course I know about Coué," Kaptchuk told me. "'I'm getting better day by day . . .'" He agreed the migraine study could coalesce with Coué's observations.

Frontiers of Thought

Have you noticed that when something is impressed upon your mind—such as a deeply held conviction, an intense yearning, or a sense of forward-looking confidence (or the opposites of any of these things)—you tend to discover connections, examples, and possibilities that seem to draw you closer to what you are focused on?

It is theoretically possible that one of the reasons a focused thought brings you in proximity to related conditions and people is not simply that you are more aware of relevant circumstances, or are willfully seizing upon confirmations of a pre-determined idea (a phenomenon called "confirmation bias"). Rather, you may be communicating your attitudes in a not yet understood extra-physical fashion to people who may be able to offer assistance, meet you halfway, or provide a necessary piece of information.

Beginning in the early 1930s, Duke University researcher JB Rhine conducted hundreds of thousands of trials, eventually spanning decades, in which subjects attempted to "guess" which card was overturned on a five-suit deck consisting of images such as a circle, square, or cross. These were called Zener cards. Certain individuals made small but statistically relevant "hits" at a higher than average rate. Rhine labored intensively, and under the scrutiny of critics, to safeguard against every form of corruption in his data, so much so that his card experiments far exceeded the controls of most clinical trails. These few percentage points of deviation, tracked across years of trials, indicated some form of anomalous transfer of information in a laboratory setting—either that, or the manner in which we compile clinical statistics is flawed in some way that we do not yet understand.

Rhine's lab work has attracted decades of controversy, but his data and research have never been overturned. Napoleon Hill and his key collaborator and benefactor, insurance executive W. Clement Stone, took this topic very seriously, as do I. Warren Weaver, a former president of the American Association for the Advancement of Science, who directed the allocation of hundreds of millions of dollars in medical research grants for the Rockefeller Foundation and Alfred P. Sloan Foundation, examined Rhine's methodology and concluded: "I cannot reject the evidence and I cannot accept the conclusions." Weaver did not share Rhine's views, but as an authentic scientist he refused to close the door on the matter.

I don't want any reader of this book to take my word or Rhine's word that this research is valid. Don't take W. Clement Stone's word—though he thought highly enough of Rhine's work to fund his lab at Duke. Research the topic yourself if it is of interest to you. It would surpass the scope of this book to consider the various implications of Rhine's experiments. For our purposes here, suffice to say: Many thoughtful, seasoned people report remarkable hunches, deeply meaningful coincidences, and fortuitous "accidents," some of which occur in ways that cannot always be defined by ordinary experience or statistical probability.

The mind is an extraordinary frontier. When you are enthusiastically and diligently focused on a desired goal, your mental apparatus sets into motion a remarkable, and not always evident, array of forces.

ACTION STEP:
The Right Way to Use Affirmations

A persistent and, I think, misdirected debate runs through the culture of self-help and positive thinking: Should affirmations be rendered in the present tense ("I am") or future tense ("I will")? Some argue that the future tense pushes off your aims to an unrealized point in time, and perpetuates current circumstances.

Is there a "right" way to affirm?

The truth is: You should use whatever language feels most authentic and natural, and helps sustain your emotive passion. When your mind is charged with an idea or image, you tend to seek circumstances that will bring it about. The key issue is focus. If you have difficulty believing that you possess something right now, and it feels more persuasive to locate it in the future, then do so. May traditionalists forgive me: There is no wrong way of affirming a goal.

The life of bestselling science-fiction novelist Octavia Butler (1947-2006) is a case in point. Butler grew up in a working-class, African-American household in Pasadena, California, in the 1950s and 60s. Awkward, shy, and unusually tall for her age, Butler felt isolated from other kids. In her solitude, she developed voracious reading habits, and a burning desire to write. Butler went on to become Sci-Fi's first widely recognized African-American woman writer, winning popularity and acclaim.

Archivists at the Huntington Library in Los Angeles discovered among the novelist's papers an extraordinary and prescient rendering of her personal vision, which Butler handwrote in 1988 in the classic tones of positive-mind metaphysics: "I shall be a bestselling writer . . . This is my life. I write bestselling novels . . . I will find the way to do this. So be it! See to it!" Butler freely used both future and present tenses in her vision. She wrote her feelings without getting distracted by form.

Butler's manifesto expressed another positive-mind principle: purposeful success. "I will send poor black youngsters to . . . writer's workshops. I will help poor black youngsters broaden their horizons . . . I will get the best of health care for my mother and myself."

You can examine Butler's handwritten affirmation for yourself online, including at Verso, the blog of the Huntington Library. Butler crafted the perfect declaration of an artist or entrepreneur expressing the language of desire.

TAKEAWAY POINTS:

- Do not assume that you already know what your aim is. We often repeat things to ourselves that do not capture our most deep-seated attitudes. Scrutinize yourself.

- Life does not bargain with us: We are given the opportunity to attain one definitely focused and passionately felt aim—not a plethora of conflicting aims or vague desires.

- An aim is much more than a mere preference or a generalized wish. It is a specific, definite, and passionately felt drive.

- A Definite Chief Aim (DCA) must have intense emotions at the back of it.

- Your aim must be specific. The more specialized it is, the more likely you are to achieve it.

- Your aim should be generative—it should provide something of concrete value to other individuals.

- Affirmations charge the mind with a distinct keenness and awareness that directs you toward opportunities to act on your goal.

- You can alter your attitudes and the actual neural activity of your brain through autosuggestion and the insights of neuroplasticity.

- Practice affirmations in the moments just before drifting to sleep at night and just as you're coming to wakefulness in the morning. Your mind is especially impressionable at such times.

• Affirmations or meditations work best at influencing the subconscious when they are sincere and emotive. Don't get hung up on language. There is no wrong way to affirm.

• We are only at the threshold of understanding the potentials of the mind. Take seriously the power and implications of thought.

2

How to Know What You (Really) Want

As we've explored, it is vital for your success—and for the avoidance of depleting distractions—to throw yourself behind one passionately held aim. This does not mean neglecting your health or home life. In fact, if you pay insufficient attention to these things you will suffer, as will those you love.

Philosopher Jacob Needleman once told me: "If you don't give something its proper attention now, it will take all of your attention later." This statement contains an extraordinary truth. Strive for balance: do not neglect health, home, intimacy, family, and so on, or these things will morph into crises that will one day steal all of your attention.

Take this caution seriously. But, at the same time, let's not be sentimental: For all the talk you may hear that "no one on his death bed wishes he had spent more time at the office"—well . . . I'm not so sure. Maybe not always the office, per se, but the studio, the workshop, the stage, the laboratory, the athletic field, the store, and, yes, *sometimes* the office.

We often hear that success cannot void other problems in our lives or compensate for poor self-image. But I challenge whether that is strictly true. Work is deeply meaningful to people. And some forms of success can be understood as productive and legitimate outgrowths, if not justifications, of struggles that we encountered early in life.

Napoleon Hill tells the story of his son, Blair, who was born in 1913 with a severe hearing disability. Across years, and through arduous effort, Hill discovered that his son did possess some hearing ability. But hearing-aid technology was then in its infancy, and no hearing aids worked satisfactorily for Blair. He honed other skills and abilities as best he could. At age 24 in 1937, the same year that *Think and Grow Rich* came out, Blair received an experimental hearing aid, which finally worked for him. The experience was like that of salvation.

"It occurred to him," Hill wrote, "that he might be of help to the millions of deafened people who go through life without the benefit of hearing devices." Blair intensively "analyzed the entire marketing system of the manufacturer of the hearing device, and created ways and means of communicating with the hard of hearing all over the world." Blair put into writing a two-year plan and was hired by the device's manufacturer.

Should someone have told Blair Hill not to work so hard? Or relax and take time to smell the roses? Of course not. Blair had a mission, a vocation, that made him feel alive—that filled him with a sense of purpose and direction. Not only that, but the experience of bringing hearing aids to the disabled brought a sense of purpose to the suffering that he had experienced up to that point in his life. (If you doubt that having a sense of purpose can ameliorate suffering, read psychologist and Holocaust survivor Viktor Frankl's book *Man's Search for Meaning*.) Blair's Definite Chief Aim was to bring new hearing technologies to the public, and thus open new possibilities for the deaf. He dedicated himself to this task with evangelical zeal.

I wish the same sense of mission for you and everyone reading this book. It is wonderful to find a task or aim that employs all of your passions. My brother-in-law switched careers from law to investment banking. He was determined to make his way in a demanding new career, which he was entering at a slightly later age than some of his colleagues. The financial rewards were great—but so were the hours and competition. One day a couple of my great aunts told him, "You shouldn't work so hard." He looked at them quizzically and asked, "Why shouldn't I work hard?" They had no idea how to respond. How can you tell a person where to direct his life's energies? If a task or aim attracts you, that is cause for cheer. It signals that you are using all of your creative and intellectual faculties. You are fulfilling your human potential.

Recall the earlier passage from *Revelation*. Life does not reward the lukewarm. If your commitment is lukewarm, so will your rewards be—at best. Some of us may depart from life feeling that we didn't press hard enough on the pedal of our desire. Does that sound like it might be you? If so, finding the right DCA now will help you avoid future regrets.

Follow Your Bliss

Here is a simple exercise that will allow you to begin the all-important process of finding and refining your DCA. Do it even if you think you already know what you want. The world-famous mythologist Joseph Campbell credited this exercise with steering him into an academic career that resulted in his becoming one of the last century's best-known scholars of myth. Campbell's analyses of heroes and mythology later inspired the work of *Star Wars* creator George Lucas, leading to archetypal characters like the young adept Luke Skywalker and the tormented villain Darth Vader.

Just before the Great Depression, Campbell was living in New York City. Pushing thirty, the not-so-young seeker was adrift: He had no idea what he wanted to do with his life. On Sundays, Campbell attended a New Thought church presided over by a minister named Fenwicke Holmes. Fenwicke was the brother and collaborator of Ernest Holmes, one of the architects of "the power of positive thinking" and the founder of *Science of Mind* magazine. Campbell approached Fenwicke for advice. The minister gave him an exercise to discover where he should direct his energies in life: "One should jot down notes for a period of four or five weeks on the things that interest one. It will be found that all the interests tend in a certain direction." This simple technique solidified Campbell's wish to study mythology.

The exercise later echoed in Campbell's famous apho-rism: "Follow your bliss."

Get a small notebook that fits comfortably in your pocket and carry it with you for several weeks, making little notes about everything that attracts you. Be dili-gent. Overlook nothing. What direction do your notes travel in? Don't prejudge what you will find. Allow your-self to be surprised.

The Three-Step Miracle

What if a genie promised you a wish, but with a catch: You had to tell him the truth about what you *really* wanted—otherwise you'd lose everything.

As noted earlier, we repeatedly tell ourselves what we want to believe ("I like my work," "I enjoy being around others," etc.), and these things take on a habit-ual, by-the-numbers quality. Yet we rarely submit our desires and wishes to mature, sustained scrutiny. Sur-prisingly often, *we do not really know what we want from life.*

Here is an extremely powerful, yet simple, exercise that will that will help you arrive at and sharpen your DCA. It may bring you serious surprises, or it may vali-date and refine your current aim. I call it the Three-Step Miracle. Try it and see if you think I'm exaggerating.

The exercise comes from a beguiling little book that I have given away more than a hundred copies of. It is a 28-page pamphlet, published anonymously in 1926 under the title *It Works*. The author, who identified himself only by the initials R.H.J., was, in actuality, a Chicago salesman named Roy Herbert Jarrett (1874-1937).

An avid student of metaphysics and a highly successful sales executive, Jarrett tested his theory for many years and didn't put it in a book until he was past the age of 50. (Something to make note of—your aim may require time to reach fruition.)

Many people swear by his little book, which has remained continually in print. If you've never heard of it, this may mark a turning point in your life. And if you do know the exercise I am about to describe, I hope that what I write here will return you to it with fresh eyes.

Jarrett distilled a program of creative-mind metaphysics into three exquisitely simple steps. But to benefit you must do them with total commitment—these steps work only if approached with your whole being. The key to almost every self-help book and exercise, I often tell people, is that you must approach it as if you life depends on it. The three steps are:

1. **Carefully devise a list of what you really want from life.** Revise it, rewrite it, and work on it every day. Throw your certainties out the window. You may write your list at 9 a.m. and feel certain it is correct, and then by 3 p.m. be ready to tear it up and start over. That's a sign you're doing it right. You may start writing your list and feel besieged by uncertainty, suddenly unclear on what you want— not sure if you ever really knew. You may despair. Good. Keep going. Keep rewriting and reorganizing your list day after day, until you reach a point in your heart and intellect where you feel certain that you've captured your deepest wishes.

2. **Read your list morning, midday, and night;
    think about it always.** Once you feel confident
    (and even then allow yourself a few reversals) that
    your list is a true summary of your deepest wishes,
    commit to reading it in a quiet, contemplative
    atmosphere each morning upon waking; again
    at midday; and once more just before drifting to
    sleep at night. Carry it with you in a sturdy pocket
    notebook or on a laminated index card. Make it your
    steady companion. Read it while standing on lines,
    commuting, taking an elevator—read it always.

3. **Tell no one what you are doing.** Some people
    have the most problem with this final step. Some
    of my friends used to joke that it was like taking
    the oath from the movie and novel *Fight Club*:
    "You DO NOT talk about Fight Club!" But the
    joke masked a truth. You must keep your list to
    yourself not to adopt some air of mystery, but to
    keep others—friends, relatives, coworkers—from
    making casually negative comments that shake your
    resolve (a favorite human pastime). These dreams
    belong to *you*. They are intimate, powerful, and
    extremely important. They are vital to your life and
    sense of wellbeing. Never, ever spill them to just
    anyone. Later on we will explore what Napoleon
    Hill taught about the importance of seeking help
    and information only from valid, useful sources
    and people—and assiduously avoiding opinions,
    rumors, gossip, and the cheap judgments of others.
    For our purposes in this exercise, it is vital that you

not allow your dreams to be vetted by the "peanut gallery." You know who this is: People who talk rather than act. Jealous coworkers. Friends who nurse regrets, resentments, or fears about their own choices. Know-it-all relatives. (A class for whom Napoleon Hill felt special ire.) Keep silent—there is great power in it.

Then, confidently express gratitude each time the results arrive.

That's it? Yes, that's it. How can something so simple really work? Because this exercise pushes us to do something that we *think* we do all time but rarely try: *Honestly come to terms with our innermost desires.*

Most of us drift through life lazily thinking that we want a new house, a loving mate, a better job, and so on. But the things that we repeat inside can merely mirror what we think would make us look good in the eyes of others, or what our upbringing or our peers tell us we should want. Or they may be fleeting fantasies—we want ice cream, so to speak, until the next thing catches our eye. All of this can obfuscate our deepest, most authentic yearnings. Ask yourself once more: Have you ever sat down, in a mature and sustained manner, stripped of all convention and inhibition, and probed, with unsparing honesty, what you *really* want from life?

We cannot harness any of the mental assets covered in chapter one unless we know where we want to go. When we do, we discover resources at our backs that we never knew we had. I guarantee that the Three-Step Miracle will yield surprising results.

A Note on Realism

I said that this book is for practical dreamers—and I meant it. I believe that true desires are realistic. Realism is a hallmark of authenticity. If you, as a mature and steady person, want something, the chances are good that you're not chasing a unicorn but that your inner resources are pointing you toward a valid objective.

How do you *know* if you are acting on an integral and realistic desire, something that you either possess the skills to attain, or that are you willing to work, study, and train to gain the skills for? Here is a personal example. In June of 2005, when my reignited writing career was in its early stages, I received a pivotal invitation. Obadiah Harris, the director of the Philosophical Research Society in Los Angeles—an organization founded by esoteric scholar Manly P. Hall and dedicated to the study of myth and religion—invited me to deliver a talk at the organization should I happen to be "in the neighborhood." I lived and worked in New York City and no plans to be in LA. I immediately emailed him back and said, yes, I'd be there in September. I felt, rightly, that this was a key opportunity, worth far more than the personal expense of my plane ticket and lodging (which was only slightly offset by the speaking honorarium).

There are times, especially (but not only) early in your career, when paying your own way or doing something for free is more than worth it. I knew that an engagement at this historic learning center would allow me to begin my career as a speaker in earnest, and would give me a podium from which to explore my ideas in front of a live audience. If you want to be a writer, artist, politician, or any kind of a publicly engaged figure, it is vital that you begin reaching an audience. For one thing, when you speak before an audience you not only test out the persuasiveness of your ideas but, if you are well prepared (and you should never step in front of an audience without being prepared), you discover new connections and angles on your own topic. The very act of articulating your ideas helps further ones to emerge, as if from the ether. As a publisher, when I receive a proposal from someone who has made no previous effort to reach an audience, however small, I am leery. The worth, sturdiness, and refinement of your ideas can come only through public airing.

I delivered a talk called The Occult Philosophy in America—by "occult" I do not mean anything sinister. Rather I am referring to a wide range of Greek-Roman-Egyptian spiritual ideas that reemerged during the Renaissance. Translators and religious scholars called them *occulta*, which is Latin for secret. In later generations some exponents of these ideas fled to the New World to avoid religious persecution, and helped lay the groundwork for a culture of religious freedom in colonial America. My talk was a success and I arrived back home in New York intending to turn a recording of it into a transcript, and from there to revise and expand it into an ambitious essay. As I began working on my project, my wife told me: "This is more than an essay or article. This is your book." I was ignited with the *rightness* of her idea. From there I began to devise a substantial (eventually 100-page) proposal for my first book, *Occult America*.

I got a literary agent who I felt ran an ethical practice, and she helped me further refine the proposal. After that she sent it out to trade publishers. Then something happened that every writer, artist, and entrepreneur must contend with: silence. Now, I am by nature a worrier. It's a burden—but it's also the quality that drove me toward the ideas of self-development. A week-plus of silence (a very short time!) had me fearful that maybe no one would want to publish my book at all. So I took a private and decisive step. One Saturday morning I got up, printed out my detailed proposal (each chapter was substantially mapped out), punched binder holes in it, and inserted it into a blue loose leaf notebook. This, I told myself, was my book in gestation—and I was going to finish it, brick by brick, whether or not I had a publisher. At that moment, I *knew* I was going to finish that book.

As it happened a major publisher, Bantam, soon got in touch and bought the book days later. The book received advance blurbs from Deepak Chopra, documentarian Ken Burns, and historian John S.D. Eisenhower (son of president Dwight Eisenhower), among others. I appeared to discuss it on CBS Sunday Morning, Dateline NBC, and NPR's All Things Considered. The book received positive reviews in *The Washington Post*, *The Boston Globe*, and *The Huffington Post*, among others. But something more important transpired on the morning that I determined, come hell or high water, *I would write that book.*

If you do not feel that kind of self-determination for a project, chances are it is the wrong one. It may not be an authentic desire, but a pipe dream—something that you fantasize about or talk about but are not sufficiently motivated, trained, and prepared to actually undertake. A friend of mine remarked that she gets tired of hearing people walk through modern-art museums, and stand before an abstract or minimalist painting and say dismissively: "I could do that!" Her response is: "No, you couldn't—but, more importantly, you wouldn't." In other words, the person who issues that challenge will never discover that he cannot, in fact, do it because he would never pick up a brush, get a canvas, dip into paints and—try. He won't. He doesn't even want to. *Never allow that to be you.* Do not hang around people who talk like that; do not disclose your dreams to them (remember step three of the Three-Step Miracle).

An authentic desire is an achievable desire. Again, you must ask yourself: Do I have the skills? Or am I prepared to make the sacrifices and exertion necessary to attain the skills? As I write these words, I am a 50-year-old man, fit and in good condition, but never much of an athlete. I am not going to be in the NBA. I am not going to join the space program. Those would be fantasies—not goals.

Are you writing a novel? Well, good—but you must be prepared to write it even if you don't find a publisher. If you are waiting for a publisher before you commence your great plan, you may not be prepared to undertake it at all. A publisher I admire once observed: "We may not be a nation of readers but we are a nation of writers." Sometimes it seems, quite literally, that more people are working on a book than reading one. Whether you are a budding novelist, screenwriter, painter, or any number of things, you must be prepared—and trained—to complete your craft without the approbation, acceptance, or remuneration of a corporate media entity.

This is true for many projects: If you are unwilling to begin, right now, and to see it through—surmounting every obstacle and wiping every tear (and there will be tears)—it may not be a realistic and authentic desire.

How can you know if your desire is realistic? Well, as noted above, the willingness and ability to begin, and to forge ahead on your own, are vital. Your age, training, and education matter—as do geography, finances, and time. These are not to be seen as barriers—but they are serious considerations. Surprises do occur: The Caribbean nation of Jamaica did, in fact, produce an Olympic bobsledding team in 1988 (as depicted in the comedy *Cool Runnings*). And some significant actors did not land the roles for which they became known until middle age. Classically trained actor Jonathan Frid was about to leave the stage and begin working as a drama coach when, at age 42, he landed the iconic role of vampire Barnabas Collins on TV's *Dark Shadows*. You may recall actor Alan Arbus as the psychiatrist Sidney Freedman on the acclaimed sit-com MASH—he got that role at age 55 after working for most of his life as a photographer. So, I am not suggesting that you retreat before barriers; but just be cognizant and realistic about where you are, what is required, and your willingness, through hard times and good, to see through your project.

In chapter five we explore the principle of "intelligent persistence"—the ethic of never giving up. There is tremendous power and validity in that. But to get to the point where you can be intelligently persistent, you must have a goal that is real, focused, and to which you are capably committed.

Let me say one further word about goals and realism. Some of my spiritual friends and colleagues have told me I am too outwardly focused. Isn't the true path, they ask, marked by a sense of non-attachment? Doesn't true awareness come from within? Isn't there finally a Higher Self or essence from which we can truly live—rather than succumb to the ersatz and illusory goals of the lower self or ego?

I have been on the spiritual path for many years. I have sought understanding within both mainstream faiths and esoteric movements. My conviction is that the true nature of life is to *be generative*. I believe that human beings should be, and in order to be happy must be, involved in exercising their fullest range of abilities. Seekers often lean too heavily on terms like "ego" or "essence," which are labels that we use to discuss matters of which we have only a foggy understanding, if that. We import concepts from Eastern religions, such as "nonattachment" and "nonidentification," which reach us through translations of translations, often many times removed from their original source.

The inner search and the search for meaning are of extraordinary importance—and are matters of extraordinary mystery. But I believe that the simplest and most resounding truth on the matter can be found in the dictum of Christ: "Render unto Caesar what is Caesar's and render unto God what is God's." We are products of both worlds, the seen and the unseen; and there is no reason to suppose that our efforts or energies are better employed in one or the other. Both exist. What's more,

I am frankly unsure that "nonattachment" is a viable path for those of us raised in the West, and elsewhere. I believe that the ethical pursuit of achievement and attainment holds greater depth, and summons more from within our inner natures, than we may understand.

Do not be afraid of your aims, or slice and dice them with melancholic pondering. Find them—and act on them. By living as an ethical, productive being, in the fullest sense, you honor the nature and gift of your existence.

"I Can Do That"

When searching for your Definite Chief Aim, I want you to watch for special moments in life when you witness someone doing something remarkable, and from a place deep within you think: "I can do that." Many artists, public speakers, writers, and high-achievers experience a crucial moment in their lives when they see someone preaching, performing, or expressing some form of art or entertainment, and they seriously and maturely say to themselves: "I can do that."

One of the most popular and widely travelled Pentecostal ministers of the twentieth century, Tommy L. Osborn, had an experience like that at age 23. In 1946, the Oklahoma-born Osborn returned from India after a disappointing year of unsuccessful missionary work. Ill from travel and depressed, Osborn took a pulpit at a small church in northern Oregon. He had doubts about continuing his ministerial career. One night in 1947 the famed evangelist William Branham held a revival campaign in nearby Portland. Urged to attend by his wife,

Osborn sat in the audience. He was electrified by the power and style of Branham, who spoke in persuasive and mesmerizing tones to rows of worshippers.

"When I witnessed this," Osborn wrote, "there seemed to be a thousand voices speaking to me at once, all in accord saying over and over, 'You can do that.'"

The following spring Osborn started his own independent ministry and became one of the most active evangelists of the century, holding tent revival meetings in fields and stadiums, and eventually travelling the world hosting some of the century's largest evangelical crusades. While flamboyant and sometimes controversial, Osborn was no mere showman. His ministry was marked by a "moral seriousness" in the words of historian David Edwin Harrell, Jr. At age 23, Osborn had felt dejected and uncertain—until one night he experienced the style of ministering that suited him best.

It would be difficult to imagine a more culturally opposite figure from Osborn than rock singer and songwriter Patti Smith. But the punk pioneer had a similar moment of awakening. At age 21 in 1968 Smith was working at a bookstore in Manhattan. She went with some friends one night to see the Doors at the Fillmore East on New York's Lower East Side. What she thought would be just another night out turned into an artistic epiphany. She wrote in her memoirs:

> I had a strange reaction watching Jim Morrison. Everyone around me seemed transfixed, but I observed his every move in a state of cold hyper-awareness. I remember this feeling much more clearly than the concert. I felt, watching Jim

Morrison, that I could do that. I can't say why I thought this. I had nothing in my experience to make me think that would ever be possible, yet I harbored that conceit.

Smith soon found her voice as a poet, playwright, journalist, and performance artist. The last of these roles lead to her mid-seventies emergence as a bracingly original rock vocalist and songwriter. She was later inducted into the Rock and Roll Hall of Fame.

Bestselling novelist Dan Brown also described an I-can-do-that moment. While working as an English teacher and trying to hone his own writing style, Brown dissected thrillers by novelists Robert Ludlum and Sidney Sheldon. While on vacation in Tahiti in 1994 he discovered a dog-eared Sheldon paperback that someone had left behind on a dock.

"It had lots of twists and turns," Brown recalled. "I thought, wow, that's exciting. Maybe I can write something like that!" Brown described a similar experience when reading a Robert Ludlum novel, and thinking he could produce the same kind of book. In analyzing the framework of these popular novelists he found that he could echo their approach. "What really helps create pace," he said, "is to have, at the heart of your novel, two enormous forces in conflict, and have your hero, ideally, getting crushed in the middle."

My own I-can-do-that moment arrived in February 2005 when I published a historical article on metaphysical philosopher Neville Goddard (1905-1972) in *Science of Mind* magazine. When I had previously interviewed pitcher Barry Zito for *Science of Mind* he remarked at a certain point: "You must be really into Neville" (who wrote under his first name). I had never heard of Neville. Barry was incredulous. I immediately got a copy of Neville's book *Resurrection*—and was enraptured. One of the most radical and eloquent thinkers from the positive-mind tradition, Neville taught that the human imagination is God, and that everything we think and feel is out-pictured into creation.

I began researching Neville, who grow up in an Anglican family in Barbados. I encountered more questions than answers in his background, but eventually was able to piece together a biographical portrait of this enigmatic figure. My article, "Searching for Neville Goddard," met with enthusiastic reader response, and was later reprinted as the introduction to an anthology of Neville's writing. I am convinced that what you can produce on a micro scale you can repeat on a macro scale. Once I had published this effective historical piece on Neville, I knew that I could write on a larger scale about the lives and ideas of other metaphysical thinkers. The article's publication set me on track as a historian of alternative spirituality, and primed me for my first book *Occult America* (indebting me once more to the Zito family). That article was my I-can-do-that moment.

Where is your I-can-do-that moment? Don't take that question lightly—and don't be glib about it. All achievement is a marriage of idealism and great execution. The *wanting* alone is insufficient—there must be impeccable follow through. But the journey can begin—and sometimes must begin—with that one spark of inner realization in which you say to yourself: *I can do that.* Watch carefully for that moment.

ACTION STEP:
How to Read a Self-Help Book

Reading quality self-help and inspirational literature is a foundational part of finding your definite aim—if you are reading this book you probably already have a sense of that.

I consider self-help a noble pursuit. Authentic self-help demands personal excellence; the overcoming of addiction or crippling habits; and striving to make life a little better for those who come near you. Some of the greatest exponents of self-help include therapist and Holocaust survivor Viktor Frankl; Alcoholics Anonymous founder Bill Wilson; and Transcendentalist philosopher Ralph Waldo Emerson, who intended his essays as practical philosophy. While the term didn't exist in his day, Benjamin Franklin can be considered a self-help writer for his popular tracts on good conduct. ("Early to bed and early to rise . . .")

Most of the self-help books that I personally read and recommend are what might be considered "golden oldies." Some of the classics, such as *The Power of Positive Thinking* and *Psycho-Cybernetics*, contain most of the wisdom that underlies the overall self-help field.

A request from a friend made me want to provide a few guidelines for getting the most out of classic self-help books. My close and longtime friend worked as a prosecutor in a large city, and asked for my help in broadening and expanding his vision of his job. As a principled law-enforcer, my friend was not content simply to "put away bad guys" (who were often poor and unable to afford good legal representation). He also wanted to address the iniquities of our justice system.

I urged him to read David J. Schwartz's 1959 classic, *The Magic of Thinking Big*. I felt he could benefit from Schwartz's message of expanding one's sense of possibilities. But my friend had rarely considered, or taken seriously, New Thought or self-help literature—so I offered a few pointers to avoid his getting lost on the way. The four principles below can help anyone, newcomers or old timers, gain the maximum benefit from literature of self-development.

1. **Do not get distracted by hackneyed language.** Many of the classics use gender stereotypes and predictably dated references. Most pioneers in New Thought and spiritual therapeutics were ardently liberal for their times; some were visionary social reformers. Nonetheless, these writers could also lean on now-dated vernacular and inferences of their era. You'll occasionally stumble on a softly bigoted reference. Pay attention to the universal message, not the attitudes of past.

2. **Never think "I get it."** When reading vintage self-help books you may encounter insights and ideas that seem familiar, or that provoke a been-there-done-that reaction in you. If

you come across things like the Golden Rule
or positive-mind aphorisms, don't roll your
eyes and start skimming. Rather, take it as
an opportunity to revisit great and powerful
truths that we might take for granted today. As
will be seen, the Golden Rule has deep layers
of meaning. Often our biggest mistake in life is
undervaluing the familiar.

3. **Do the exercises**. It's always tempting to save
   the exercises "for later." That often means
   never doing them at all. Even if you've tried
   something before (such as writing down a list
   of goals), or if a technique seems burdensome
   (such as a daily meditation practice), the rule
   is: DO IT ANYWAY. If you really want to get
   something out of a self-improvement program
   you must dedicate yourself to its details. There
   may be shortcuts in life—but they do not
   include skipping the exercises.

4. **The secret to self-help**. There is a "secret
   law" behind every self-help program. Without
   this law, nothing is possible. It is: *Do the
   program as if your life depends on it.* I mean it.
   If you proceed that way, things will happen.
   Almost any sound program works *if* you
   commit to it with absoluteness. Select your
   book or program—and then burn the fleet.
   Give yourself no way out. Throw yourself
   into it with passionate, obsessive intensity.
   Life rewards no mediocre efforts. An Arab

proverb goes, "The way bread smells depends on how hungry you are." Be starved for self-improvement. Passion delivers you.

And what happened to my friend who wanted to expand his work in law enforcement? He soon got a state-level job investigating fatal police shootings of unarmed civilians. His determination to be fair, principled, and dogged in pursuit of justice took him to a position of high responsibility.

The Psychology of Clothing

Can you prime yourself to awaken to your life's purpose? Here is a simple factor that will help. When searching for your aim in life, the daily manner in which you dress and present yourself can actually make a difference. Being comfortable and at home in your own skin makes you more confident, alert, and helps to attract the right kind company and colleagues.

The first time I "took a meeting" (as Hollywood people say) at a media hot spot in New York City I was worried that I'd be underdressed. But when I arrived, I discovered that all the men were dressed like fifteen-year-old boys. I fit right in. I wear hoodies, jeans, sneakers, and t-shirts. I'm not trying to affect a "look"—it's just what makes me comfortable. And this points to an important truth about the psychology of clothing.

Religious ethics teach that change begins within, and that we shouldn't be overly concerned with outer appearances. "By their fruits ye shall know them," Jesus said. But that does not mean that the inner world is the only one in which we function: there is a subtle interplay between inner and outer. If you want to get a running start on healthful self-confidence, your outer appearance makes a significant difference.

Past generations were told to "dress for success"—which often meant suits and shined shoes for men, and professional dresses or pants suits for women. But today's secret to dressing for success is adopting a daily "uniform" that makes you feel self-possessed and at home wherever you are. That doesn't mean wearing flip-flops to a funeral or an "I Brake for Beer" t-shirt on a job interview. But it does mean taking the chance of being wholly you.

Napoleon Hill emphasized this point in his 1928 *The Law of Success*: "An appearance of prosperity attracts attention, with no exceptions whatsoever. Moreover, a look of prosperity attracts 'favorable attention,' because the one dominating desire in every human heart is to be prosperous."

I would update Hill's advice by substituting the word "independence" for "prosperity." Today's dominating desire is to be self-directed, independent, and—yes—prosperous.

Do you recall what Steve Jobs chose as Apple's slogan? "Think Different." Jobs wore a studied daily uniform of black turtlenecks, jeans, and New Balance sneakers. His appearance said: *I make my own rules; I think different.* Jobs didn't hit on this outfit casually. When visiting Japan in the early 1980s, Jobs was impressed with how Japanese factory workers each dressed in the same crisp uniforms. He asked a world-class Japanese designer to devise a regular uniform for him. The result was literally one hundred of the same black turtlenecks. He not only felt at ease, and made a statement, but also dispensed with the time-wasting practice of selecting a new wardrobe each day.

In one of my favorite episodes of *The Simpsons*, a teacher tells young Lisa Simpson: "Being tough comes from inside. First step—change your outside." It's a joke, of course—but like most jokes it conceals truth: The outside reinforces who you are within. Take the time to think about whether you are comfortable and relaxed with what you are wearing, and how it presents you to others.

None of this means running out and spending big bucks on a new wardrobe. You can carefully select a few choice items that you wear repeatedly. Europeans are masterful at this. Years ago a family friend and successful clothing designer, Jane Hamill, attended fashion school in Paris. She noticed that one of her teachers wore the same Chanel skirt every day. Jane did not see this as eccentric or inappropriate. Rather, she found it a practical expression of good taste. The teacher preferred to wear the same impeccable skirt every day rather than wear a shoddy or poor-quality skirt. The teacher was instructing her students: It is better to be seen in one nice thing than a bunch of so-so things. In Rome some cab drivers (the best ones) wear tailored suits and contoured sunglasses. They look impeccable all the time, even though they may own only a couple of such suits.

There are still more benefits to a daily uniform. A rock critic once said that he dressed every single day in a black suit and black t-shirt. It prepared him for any outing, nighttime event, or meeting. President Obama said that during his presidency he restricted his mode of dress to either a blue or gray suit so that, like Steve Jobs, he never had to waste time deciding what to wear. "You need to focus your decision-making energy," Obama said of his wardrobe. "You need to routinize yourself. You can't be going through the day distracted by trivia." Hoodie-wearing Internet magnate Mark Zuckerberg has made a similar observation.

The point is not to be vain or excessively concerned with your outer appearance. The objective is simply to feel your best. When you do, you are more relaxed, attractive, and personable. When you are comfortable you also act and think more adroitly. You are better primed to discover and move toward your Definite Chief Aim.

Right Where You Stand

In certain cases you already may be acting on your Definite Chief Aim without realizing it. My friend Christina Reinwald owns and operates a beloved children's hair salon in Brooklyn, NY, called Rockin' Locks. (Okay, full disclosure: she cuts my hair, too—I am the world's biggest kid.) Christina is a remarkable stylist, with a serious rock-and-roll aesthetic and a vision of what looks best on each client. What's more, she is great in dealing with kids, including my two sons. While kids generally squirm or even cry (when very young) during haircuts, Christina is someone that kids look up to and look forward to visiting. She has an uncanny knack for drawing kids into conversation about things that really matter to them. Rarely is there a squirm in sight.

Although Christina was always dedicated to her work and entrepreneurship as a stylist, for a time she balanced haircutting with attending school to become a special-education teacher, a job that one could easily see her being attracted to. But after some searching—and a very special question—Christina discovered that she was already on her path of purpose. I'll let her explain:

I had been working in a children's salon for a few years and decided that I wanted to go to school to (finally) be a teacher for early childhood and special education. I would work in the salon five days a week and attend Brooklyn College two days a week. I was also required to do field work, like going into classrooms to get the "teacher" experience. As I was doing fieldwork in multiple schools, working in the salon, going to class, and, on top of all that, going to clients' homes freelance, I consistently asked myself if I really wanted to be a teacher. During my time doing fieldwork I started a mental checklist: a "no" column and a "yes" column. I found I had more checkmarks in the "no" column than the "yes" column. Again, this led me to question whether I really wanted to be a teacher.

Then, I started to ask my clients, the parents, when they knew what they truly wanted to do. It took one of my clients –only one of them—to ask me: "What makes you happy?" That's when I knew that I was already doing what I was sup-posed to do! I was totally in my element cutting kids' hair. I was already being my authentic self!

Today, I am running my own business, a kids' salon. I love doing my job every day, so that school seems like it was centuries ago!

"What makes you happy?" came as a serious and pivotal question because it didn't direct Christina to some faraway unicorn, but, in this case, to exactly where she was standing. We all ask ourselves what makes us happy—but it can be an idle question. When it is asked with deep seriousness, however, and combined with your aptitudes and training (or training that you can acquire), it becomes more penetrating. Wherever you are in life, chances are you've already invested a lot to be there. It is possible that your current skills, perhaps with some adjustment (in Christina's case it came with owning her own salon), have placed you on exactly the right path.

As you're searching for your DCA, consider all of your options. Including the possibility that you're already doing the right thing.

ACTION STEP:
Your Week of Wonder

I firmly believe that small steps—taken with dedicated passion—can lead to great things. In that vein, I dare you to spend exactly one week exposing yourself, in mind, body, and spirit, to life's most noble things.

Not necessarily the most expensive things—that would miss the point. But rather seek to enjoy things in literature, art, music, and philosophy that have proven power of posterity and value. When altering your "diet" in this way you may invite changes into your life, or generate flashes of inspiration, which can prove beneficial in finding and acting on your Definite Chief Aim.

This exercise is from an overlooked motivational masterpiece *I Dare You* written in 1931 by William H. Danforth, the founder of the Ralston Purina Company. He wrote:

Dare to live in the Presence of the Best. Try for one week to live a distinguished life, surrounding yourself with the very best the world has to offer. Read an excellent poem. Begin the biography of a distinguished man. Study a painting by an Old Master . . . Listen to a classical radio program or a symphony. See an uplifting play or movie. Hear from a stirring speaker. Meet an inspiring personality. See a sunrise and a sunset. Strive to crowd out of your life unworthy thoughts, unworthy acts, unworthy contacts. Just see what will happen if, for a solid week, you fill your life only with the best!—the very best in literature, the very best in art, the very best in nature.

Here are my suggestions for your "Week of Wonder:"

- Read the biography of a visionary. I recommend *Steve Jobs* by Walter Isaacson.
- Enroll in a class or workshop that gets you using your mind and body, such as martial arts, yoga, or sculpting.

- Walk as many places as possible. Take a different route to work, home, and friend's homes.
- Experience politics from an outlook different than your own. Read a book that runs counter to your own viewpoints by serious authors such as laissez-faire capitalist Ayn Rand or democratic socialist Michael Harrington.
- Listen to Prokofiev's Piano Concerto No. 1. Listen to Beethoven's Ninth Symphony.
- Experience modern classical music, such as John Adams' opera *Nixon In China*.
- Watch movies that demonstrate different forms of persistence, such as *It's a Wonderful Life*; *A Most Violent Year*; and *Miracle*.
- Read Ralph Waldo Emerson's essays *Self-Reliance*, *Compensation*, and *Spiritual Laws*.
- Take a day by yourself to visit a new city—go to the museum, the library, and local historical or culture spots. If you cannot get away for a day, use a lunch hour to visit a historical site or museum nearby.
- Use your hands: plant something or work on a crafts project, such as the restoration of an antique.
- If you watch television, watch series of quality, such as *Brideshead Revisited*, *Parade's End*, or *Show Me a Hero*.
- Begin a great novel, such as George Orwell's 1984, Jane Austen's *Pride and Prejudice*, or even Bram Stoker's *Dracula*.

"But I Don't Have an Aim"

From time to time I hear from people who insist that they simply have no goal. "I've searched," someone once wrote me, "but I don't have an aim."

Personally, I don't buy that.

I extended an offer to the person who wrote me. Try the Three-Step Miracle, I said, then write back to tell me how it went, and we'll find your aim together. "Great!" he replied. I never heard another word.

People sometimes want little more than pleasures and security from life; and when those things fail, they start looking for something bigger—only to reverse themselves when game tickets or a night out drinking beckons, or when an old flame comes back into their lives, or some such. They accept a challenge only to abandon it when another shiny object catches their eye.

I have a good friend who is a meditation teacher. He told me that people sometimes complain to him that they would love to learn to meditate but they can't afford the class fee. He offers to teach such people for free—all he asks is that the person first write him a letter saying why he wants to learn to meditate. "Not more than one in ten people ever write me that letter," he told me. This is typical of human nature.

People often say that they "would write," "would meditate," "would get straight As," if only some factor weren't standing it their way. This is often little more than a ruse we play on ourselves. Most of the time we do exactly what we want to do. Which, frankly, is often nothing. Or the bare minimum necessary to take home a paycheck and entertain ourselves during off-hours. That is no way to live. It leads to poor health, depression, and ennui. It can also push people to take dangerous risks to fill holes in their lives.

If you find that the exercises in this book are doing nothing for you, I ask you to consider whether you *want* to find an aim. Or, frankly, whether social media, another beer, a bag of chips, fantasy sports—name your anesthetic—is pretty much all that you want from life. I'm not knocking any of those things. I like a relaxing evening having a beer and watching an episode of *Star Trek*. We all need to unwind, and kicking back is a healthy part of life. But if your life is limited to the 9-to-5 workday and a few hours of escapism, then inertia can overtake you. I am convinced that human beings are built to be purposeful. To be otherwise is to betray your deepest nature. If this weren't true, bridges would never have been built, oceans never crossed, and cures, vaccines, and medications never discovered.

People often remain inert because they are more fearful of criticism or humiliation than they are desirous of success. Some people are so frightened by the prospect of falling flat and experiencing humiliation (or what they think will be humiliation) that they find it safer to do nothing. They are sometimes unaware of this downward gravitational pull. I had a friend like that in college. He would hang around on the fringes of art scenes, music scenes, and film scenes—always playing it cool and wanting to know where the after-party was. But he never stepped into the arena himself. He never tried his hand at any of the cultural expressions that animated life in his social circle. He was so fully invested in maintaining his own "insider" image that he was afraid of putting himself out there, and possibly stumbling.

"*The fear of criticism in such cases is stronger than the DESIRE for success,*" Napoleon Hill wrote.

If you are afraid of criticism or self-exposure I can tell you from experience that it is far better to allow fear to *push you to prepare* than to remain on the sidelines. Nothing is ultimately sadder than a life lived on the sidelines. Fear can be a form of excitement that drives you to stay up all night studying, reworking your business plan, or rerunning the numbers on your financial product.

In the 2014 movie *A Most Violent Year* actor Oscar Isaacs brilliantly portrays an intensely driven New York businessman named Abel Morales. Abel strives to run his heating-oil company ethically and successfully while being plagued by the hijacking of his trucks and other serious forms of harassment. Someone challenges him: "And you don't get scared?" Abel replies: "I've always been a lot more afraid of failure than of anything else." In another scene a friend asks Abel what's behind his obsessive ambitions: "Why do you want it so much?" Abel replies earnestly: "I have no idea what you mean." To him achievement is life itself. Watch the movie. Study his character's determination. Learn from it.

I attended the Long Island High School for the Arts. My drama teacher, Bert Michaels, a highly successful actor in his own right, used to say that when you are rehearsing a song or monologue that you intend to use in auditions "you have to do it over and over and over again, until the point where if you hear it one more time you're going to kill yourself. Then do it one more time." Determination and fear are remarkably similar—*but only if they are used toward productive ends*. Be as scared as you want. Don't fight it. But channel the fear into building armor around yourself in the form of preparation, drilling, and determination. Do that and you will not only feel ready to face the tests that will come, but you will feel a new sense of self-respect. You will feel purposeful. And this won't be fantasy, but lived fact.

After emigrating from Soviet Russia to Hollywood in the 1920s, novelist and philosopher Ayn Rand struggled as a young screenwriter, often not having enough to eat. She wrote notes in her journal to discipline herself: "From now on, no thought whatever about yourself, only about your work. You don't exist. You're only a writing engine." Does that sound extreme? It is not. It is the type of determination that scales barriers.

Humanity is not going to rid itself of fear, insecurity, or self-doubt anytime soon. These are innate traits. Rather, allow your fear or uncertainty to prod you to prepare rather than to run and hide. That includes the kind of hiding that occurs behind the TV remote. The motto of Temple University is: *Perseverance Conquers*. I have literally never seen a persistent, hardworking businessperson, artist, or athlete *permanently* fail. Never. Their plans may have worked out differently than they had foreseen. They may have had to make serious adjustments in life. But they were delivered to some sense of satisfaction and achievement.

TAKEAWAY POINTS:

- Let no one set your priorities for you. Whatever you love doing—whether done in the office, studio, or stage—is your truth. There is rarely such thing as working "too hard."

- Your traumas and difficulties in life can legitimately fuel your drive to achieve. Allow your struggles to push you.

- Write down everything that interests you for several weeks. You will notice important patterns.

- Do the Three-Step Miracle—even if you think you already know your aim. Do it with total commitment.

- Never underestimate the power of writing down your aim.

- These exercises are not about chasing unicorns. You must match your aptitudes to your aim. You must understand what training is required.

- Do not be thrown off your aim by needless ponderings. Meaning in life comes from being a generative, productive human being pursuing an ethical aim.

- Watch for that special moment when you see someone doing something at the peak of his abilities, and you say within: *I can do that.*

- Avail yourself of excellent motivational literature. Never be ashamed to be a "self-help junkie." Self-help is a noble calling.

- Your appearance affects your psychology and confidence. Do not just "dress for success," but dress for comfort and a feeling of self-possession. It matters.

- Consider that you may the doing the thing you love right now. Never overlook your current achievements—you may be exactly where you belong.

- Take a "Week of Wonder" to explore new possibilities in life.

- Never let yourself off the hook by concluding that you have no aim. That is the language of inertia, fear, and future regrets.

3

But Is It Good?

You may think that this is a chapter you can skip. But in retrospect you will likely find it the most important chapter in this book. No one likes being told to "be good." I don't. But there is sound reason to ensuring that your Definite Chief Aim—and, hence, your life—is directed toward higher ethics, and toward helping others attain their own highest good. In fact, if you ever feel stuck in your career, your goals, or in the things that you wish to actualize in life, or if you are having difficulty formulating your DCA, you must examine your relationship to the Golden Rule.

The ethic of "doing unto others" is so familiar that we think it belongs to childhood lessons, or see it as a benign truism like "early to bed, early to rise" that holds no insight for serious people. Yet there is an unseen dimension to the Golden Rule that is so powerful that you will receive an entirely new assessment of your life when you realize what it means.

The Inner Golden Rule

Shortly before I began writing this book, I felt that an unnamed *something* was stymying my progress toward my DCA. Something was limiting my ability to envision and pursue higher possibilities. I was stuck in a holding pattern.

I found the answer to my predicament in a passage from Napoleon Hill's 1928 *The Law of Success*. The key to my problem was the Golden Rule. The precept "do unto others as you would have them do unto you" appears in virtually every religious and ethical teaching, from the Talmud to the Gospels to the Bhagavad Gita. Dubbed the Golden Rule in late-seventeenth century England, this dictum seems like it's just for Sunday school kids rather than striving adults. But the Golden Rule holds an inner truth that can make all the difference in your life.

Napoleon Hill related the Golden Rule to the phenomenon of autosuggestion, or the suggestions we continually make to ourselves. As we've seen, auto-suggestion is the tool identified by mind theorist Emile Coué; it forms the basis of many of today's placebo studies and is at the back of Coué's "day by day" mantra. What we internally repeat about ourselves takes root in our subconscious and contributes to our self-image and perceptions of the surrounding world. This is a profound and determinative fact.

But note this carefully: the autosuggestive process is also triggered by *what we think about others*.

"Your thoughts of others are registered in your subconscious mind through the principle of autosuggestion," Hill wrote, "thereby building your own character in exact duplicate." Hence: "You must *think of others as you wish them to think of you.*' The law upon which the Golden Rule is based begins affecting you, for good or evil, the moment you release a *thought*."

It is worth considering Hill's point of view more fully:

If all your acts toward others, and even your thoughts of others, are registered in your subconscious mind, through the principle of autosuggestion, thereby building your own character in exact duplicate of your thoughts and acts, can you not see how important it is to guard those acts and thoughts?

We are now in the very heart of the real reason for doing unto others as we would have them do unto us, for it is obvious that whatever we do unto others we do unto ourselves.

Stated in another way, every act and every thought you release modifies your own character in exact conformity with the nature of the act or thought, and your character is a sort of center of magnetic attraction, which attracts to you the people and conditions that harmonize with it. You cannot indulge in an act toward another person without having first created the nature of that act in your own thought, and you cannot release a thought without planting the sum and substance and nature of it in your own subconscious mind, there to become a part and parcel of your own character.

Grasp this simple principle and you will understand why you cannot afford to hate or envy another person. You will also understand why you cannot afford to strike back, in kind, at those who do you an injustice. Likewise, you will understand the injunction, "Return good for evil."

When we indulge in fantasies of revenge or score settling—which I've done during morning shaves more times than I can count—we not only shackle ourselves to past wrongs, but also to the wrongs that we would do in exchange. Our acts of violence, whether by mind, talk, or hand, reenact themselves in our psyches and perceptions. We are lowered to the level of people we resent or even hate when we counter—mentally or otherwise—their type of behavior. An adjunct to the Golden Rule could be: We become what we don't forgive.

Conversely, thoughts of generosity and forgiveness add a special solidity to our character, Hill notes, "that gives it life and power." If you struggle with forgiveness, don't worry. I deal more fully with how to approach forgiveness, and how to receive the corresponding benefits it brings, a little later in this chapter.

In sum, our thoughts about ourselves *and about others* are an invisible engine that molds our own character and experience. If you find yourself bumping against limits, or having difficulty formulating your DCA, reconsider your relationship to the Golden Rule.

The Circle of Ethics

The Golden Rule should directly inform the nature of your DCA. Your aim, to be lasting and authentic, should form a circle of ethics that benefits everyone with whom you transact. Few thinkers have spoken to this point as clearly as author Russell H. Conwell (1843-1925). Conwell belonged to a generation of late nineteenth-century motivational writers who regarded good character as the indispensible ingredient to success. Without character, the minister and educator said, worldly achievement could never bring lasting happiness.

Conwell began giving his famous motivational lecture called *Acres of Diamonds* in the 1870s, and was said to have delivered it more than 6,152 times around the nation before his death in 1925. He maintained a grueling speaking schedule not only to encourage young people in the ways of ethical achievement, but also to put his speaking fees toward the founding of a college dedicated to educating poor and working-class students. That school today is Temple University in Philadelphia.

Acres of Diamonds remains as sturdy a guide to meaningful success as when Conwell received inspiration for the lecture (and its title) while traveling as a journalist through Persia and Northern Africa in 1869. The ex-Civil War officer spent many hours (not always happily) listening to the folk tales that his Arab guides insisted on reciting for travellers. One of them was an intriguing morality tale about a wealthy Persian farmer who had squandered his money and health searching the world for diamonds—only to die a pauper before diamonds were finally discovered on the very farm that he had abandoned to embark on his quest.

The lesson that Conwell took from this story is that success can be found right where you stand—provided you possess the simplicity and soundness of character to see it. While *Acres of Diamonds* holds many lessons for today's go-getter, it differs in tone from later generations of motivational literature. Conwell insisted that sound character and sound business are innately joined: one could not exist without the other. The chief aim of the businessman, he taught, is to figure out what the people around him need, and devote himself to filling those legitimate needs. This can also make him very wealthy.

Conwell did not believe that the capitalist should fleece his customers and workers, but rather profit from them on the same scale as they profited from him. "I should sell each bill of goods," Conwell wrote, "so that the person to whom I sell shall make as much as I make." He did not necessarily mean this literally but was implying that the dollar earned should bring equal benefit or accrual to the customer. I believe that's been true for virtually every book I've published, as either an editor or author.

In 2015, *The New York Times* noted that Conwell's "famed 'Acres of Diamonds' speech fused Christianity and capitalism." That assessment is right. Conwell saw the good Christian and the good businessman as one and the same (though he noted that his ideas were for motivated people of all backgrounds).

You can take away four principles from Conwell's philosophy of ethical business:

1. Greatness is often achieved right where you are.
    (Recall the story of Christina, the stylist and salon
    owner from the previous chapter.)

2. Lasting success, including wealth, comes from *filling
    a legitimate human need.*

3. Truly exceptional people, whether entrepreneurs,
    inventors, or artists are *simple*—they are plain and
    direct in speech, methods, ideas, and inventions.

4. Money is power, greatness, and good—but only in
    the hands someone who will *use it well.*

Conwell's ideal of success—as radical today as it was in
the Victorian age—is this: If you sincerely care enough
about people to understand and provide for their needs,
you will receive material rewards, which, in turn, can be
used to uplift others. This is the circle of sound business, good ethics, and meaningful existence.

ACTION STEP:
I Believe

I recommend the following meditation on ethical
success to every working person, entrepreneur,
manager, and artist. It is adapted from the *Credo*
of early twentieth-century social reformer Elbert
Hubbard, whose work we will explore in chapter
five. Post this somewhere where you will see it regularly. Recite it. Memorize it.

I believe in myself.

I believe in the goods I sell.

I believe in my colleagues and helpers.

I believe in the efficacy of printer's ink.

I believe in producers, creators, manufacturers, distributors, and in all the workers of the world who have a job and hold it down.

I believe that truth is an asset.

I believe that the first requisite in success is not to achieve a dollar but to confer a benefit, and that the reward will come automatically and usually as a matter of course.

I believe that the greatest word in the English language is "Sufficiency."

I believe that when I make a sale I must make a friend.

I believe that when I part with you I must do it in such a way that when you see me again you will be glad—and so will I.

I believe in the hands that work, in the brains that think, and in the hearts that love.

—1912, adapted form Elbert Hubbard's *Credo*

The Midas Touch

You probably know about the Greek myth of King Midas and his "golden touch." Owed a favor by the god Dionysus, the rapacious king asked that everything he touch turn to gold. The god reluctantly granted his wish. Midas soon found himself unable even to eat as his food turned to gold. In a nineteenth-century retelling by American writer Nathaniel Hawthorne, the king embraced his daughter only for her to turn to gold. He sacrificed love and life for riches. In the Greek myth, Midas finally prays to Dionysus for mercy and the god tells him to wash himself in a river whose waters absorb his "gift," turning the pale yellow of gold, and the curse is lifted. Despising riches, Midas lives out the rest of his life in the woods.

Now, let's say that you are certain you have reached your DCA. How do know that you have arrived at the *right* wish—one that leads towards toward sustained happiness rather than the desperation of King Midas? In my many years as a publisher—and I think many of my fellow editors would agree—I've observed few things uglier than an author who wants to succeed more than he wants *to serve something good*.

Industriousness is a virtue. Narrow ambition is not. Nor is greed. Nor is the hunger to be continually celebrated or validated. Of course, without the drive to attain, to be recognized, to aspire to victory, great works of art would never be produced, diseases never cured, and the solar system never explored. But when the personal drive to excel becomes one's *chief quality*—when it surpasses all other principles and intentions—that's when feats of engineering crumble because graft overcomes workmanship.

You've heard the expression "selling out." Selling out doesn't mean going for money. There's nothing specifically wrong with that. Selling out means *placing money before quality*. I've had the privilege of publishing filmmaker David Lynch, who you may know for his television series *Twin Peaks* and his movies like *Mulholland Drive* and *Blue Velvet*. He is often credited with bridging the gap between independent art-house films and Hollywood moviemaking. The reason that people respect David, and that he is a hero to many film students and young artists, is that he has never sold out. David's genius as a director is that he is perfectly capable of writing and shooting a standard thriller; but he takes that ability and zigzags with it as his imagination requires, so that his movies are a combination of suspenseful storytelling and surrealistic dreamscapes, which get under your skin. He didn't set out to make a statement or to making a killing. He simply honors the idea. To him, fulfilling the vision is the highest ethic of a creative person in any field.

Being self-directed and working with integrity make you magnetic and attractive to people. While everyone else is trying to curry favor, the person with integrity and purpose stands out. Take careful note of this passage from Ralph Waldo Emerson:

> Let me whisper a secret; nobody ever forgives any admiration in you of them, any overestimate of what they do or have. I acquiesce to be that I am, but I wish no one to be civil to me. Strong men understand this very well. Power fraternizes with power, and wishes you not to be like him but like yourself. Echo the leaders and they will fast enough see that you have nothing for them. They came to you for something they had not. There is always a loss of truth and power when a man leaves working for himself to work for another. Absolutely speaking, I can only work for myself. All my good is magnetic, and I educate not by lessons but by going about my business.

The right aim is often accompanied by a distinctive fearlessness. An Indian youth once told the spiritual teacher Krishnamurti that he feared being kicked out of his home if he violated his father's wishes and pursued a career as an engineer. Act, the spiritual teacher told the student, and life will rise to your demands:

> If you persist in wanting to be an engineer even though your father turns you out of the house, do you mean to say that you won't find ways and means to study engineering? You will beg, go to friends. Sir, life is very strange. The moment you are very clear about what you want to do, things happen. Life comes to your aid—a friend, a relation, a teacher, a grandmother, somebody helps you. But if you are afraid to try because your father may turn you out, then you are lost. Life never comes to the aid of those who merely yield to some demand out of fear. But if you say, "This is what I really want to do and I am going to pursue it," then you will find that something miraculous takes place.

Seen from a certain perspective, the "golden touch" is integrity. If people grant us favors it is not because we kowtow to them but because we supply something within ourselves that others are naturally drawn to: it is often in the form of a quiet steadfastness, a willingness to do what is right by our own lights, and to shoulder the consequences.

Few people are willing to deal with consequences. I once published an author whose book was (rightly) in danger of cancellation due to chronic lateness. He told me in protest: "I finish what I start." But his point was irrelevant. He was already at liberty to do what he wanted, either finish or not finish. But he could not demand that someone still pay his way, and on his own schedule. (I actually did give him a break and readjusted his schedule. He never delivered.)

Courage is something you must do all by yourself. If you go your own way, you may have to face a loss here and there. But you cannot call yourself courageous while also insisting that others continue to pay you when and how much you want. I often tell people don't be a hero *after* you cash the check. But if you face a loss, consider what you gain: the reward of seeing through your own vision, and the honor of your peers.

ACTION STEP:
Take the No-Gossip Pledge

Here is an incredibly powerful step guaranteed to sharpen your mental skills and creativity. This one step will also energize, improve, and bring greater peace into your life. You will sleep better. You will experience greater self-respect. You will be more productive.

If all this could be found in a pill, what would you pay for it? This formula is free, and it can be yours immediately. Its only aftereffects are satisfaction, calm, and good spirits.

Ready to try? It comes down to two words: *Stop gossiping.*

Read those two words again. And again. Impress them upon your memory.

Acts of gossiping, tale bearing, and spreading—or listening to—rumors are a poisonous smog that clouds your life as much the lives of those who are defamed.

"But I'm only telling the truth!" we object. Not so. Virtually every rumor that we hear or repeat is untrue, half-true, or mitigated by gravely serious circumstances of which we are unaware.

The ancient Greeks cautioned to respect your neighbor's privacy: "Zeus hates busybodies," wrote the playwright Euripides. In Judaism no sin other than murder is considered worse than tale bearing or *lashon hara*, Hebrew for "evil tongue." New Thought has a similar perspective: "What man says of others will be said of him," wrote Florence Scovel Shinn. Neville Goddard taught that all talk concretizes reality, for the speaker as much as for the one spoken of.

Rejecting gossip is ever more urgent in today's world, where a huge amount of entertainment is based in smears and cruel jokes. Radio shock jocks, "reality" TV, political talk shows, snarky social media, and much of what holds our attention involves demeaning others.

By "saying no" to gossip, you not only contribute to a better home and workplace, but you *become* a nobler person.

What if just a dozen people reading these words made a no-gossip pledge and, in turn, challenged a friend or loved one to do the same—and to likewise pass along the challenge? Imagine the ripple effect.

Salesmanship and the Search for God

My friend Liam O'Malley once told me: "America is the only nation where a guide to salesmanship can lead a person to a search for God." His observation is absolutely right. The cynics will never understand why.

When a person begins to probe good self-help literature, and books on using mental visualization and autosuggestion as techniques to success, he or she inevitably begins to ask questions about the underlying laws and forces of life.

In my book *One Simple Idea,* a history and analysis of the positive-thinking movement, I made that point that not everything that happens to us is under the workings of the mind. We live under myriad laws and forces, including physical limitations, twists of fortune, and accidents. But part of what happens to us—often the most significant part—emerges from the unseen workings of our minds, emotions, and sense of self. When a person acknowledges that unseen antecedents are behind the outer events of life (which is, in a sense, the key insight of modern thought—in psychology, economics, and the sciences), he also begins to wonder about the existence and role of immaterial causes.

If universal laws and ethics exist, then it follows that at least part of what happens to us in life is rooted not only in attitudes, decisions, and insights, but perhaps in something more. If thought has a nonphysical component, whether in the form of some kind of anomalous transfer of communication between two minds or the elusive capacity of an observation or conviction to influence circumstance, then we start to the approach the question of a metaphysical dimension to life.

Indeed, if anomalous forms of communication can be demonstrated, or at least sustained as a reasonable question in a laboratory setting, and I argue that they can, it at least opens us to the possibility that the mind operates not only within the gray matter of the brain but also within a nonphysical field of activity—that our thoughts, and those of others, are part of a creative agency outside of commonly observed sensory data. This is a point of view in which Napoleon Hill took great interest.

If we surmise, or at least consider, that collective humanity participates in an immaterial intelligence, this begs the question of the existence of what Ralph Waldo Emerson termed an "Over-Soul" and Napoleon Hill called the "Master Mind"—a quality of intelligence that is greater than our individualized thoughts. The question of nonphysical intelligence leads also to the consideration of a Higher Power, or God.

The reader of this book, or any motivational guide, has urgent earthly needs, often financial. But the dedicated seeker—the person whose questions are persistent and ever deepening—will inevitably find that the quest for a "better way" in material affairs broadens to include the meaning and nature of all of life. The sincere search for a "better way" leads to questions of purpose and existence.

We "cannot serve God and mammon," Scripture tells us. But a life of seeking may lead you to a different kind of relationship with mammon, and to the questions of how to make mammon a servant rather than a master (whether in circumstances of plenty or lack), as well as to what mammon is really *for*. These questions in themselves direct the striving individual to consider how his or her DCA relates to, or results from, a higher principle of life.

My friend Liam, who I quoted above, is a case in point. He is a gifted and passionate musician, an accomplished salesman and marketer, and a dedicated seeker—his life is a crossroads of the search for the God and the question of how to live rightly in the world. Liam is someone to whom money, ethics, and seeking are one-in-the-same. There is no "inner" or "outer." It's all *one life*. These are considerations that I hope you will come to as you formulate and hone your DCA.

The Power of Forgiveness

At first glance it may seem that the topic of forgiveness has little to do with formulating and carrying out your Definite Chief Aim. But look more closely. Holding grudges and feeling deep anger toward others clouds your judgment, wastes your time in useless ruminations, and keeps you from your highest potential. Virtually every religious and ethical system in world history espouses some version of karma. The only way to be set free from painful past events and relationships is to first set others free. This is forgiveness.

If you can really, truly forgive everyone who has ever hurt you—especially those who don't seem to deserve it—you will become more effective, appealing, and possessed of unique energy and leadership ability. You will be a bigger person. And, of course, we all need forgiveness. Others resent or even hate us for things that we are not even aware of having done. But the only way to receive forgiveness is to first give it. In a certain sense, forgiveness is the sole escape hatch from your own karma; it is the one true way to reset the clock of your life.

Remember: Forgiveness is not just for others, or even primarily for others. Forgiveness rescues you. Because *what you don't forgive you become.* Do you want to be different from your bellicose coworkers, your critical parents, or your jealous tormentors? Then forgive them. Doing so will free up enormous reserves of energy to pursue what really matters: your definite aim in life. If I told you that flicking a light switch would make you 50% more effective, would you do so? Of course. That's what forgiveness is, and more. By forgiving others we are forgiven. That point is made throughout the Gospels.

Well and good to state all this—but how do we achieve it? First comes the wanting. Wanting to forgive makes it possible. You may candidly conclude that you want to, or even that you *want* to want to, but you are not emotionally ready. This is understandable. We've all been there. Human beings are not infrequently cruel and destructive, and they cause serious emotional and physical pain. Pray for guidance. Ask a Higher Power to help you see clearly and to open you to forgiveness. If you prefer not to pray, sit in meditation and consider the ethical dimensions of forgiveness: What would you would gain from it, and how would your capacity to forgive help those around you, such as your spouse or children, who would no longer feel burdened by your anger toward others?

Once you have taken these steps, I recommend that you undertake a simple, extraordinarily powerful exercise devised by my friend Richard Smoley, an acclaimed historian and spiritual philosopher. Richard described his exercise in a short, immensely potent book (which I had the pleasure to publish) called *The Deal.* As Richard puts it: "*The Deal* is this: *You agree to give up all your grievances and resentments and grudges for good. In exchange, you ask for—and receive—complete forgiveness for yourself.*"

With Richard's permission, I have abridged his nine-step exercise for this book. Please understand that this digest-sized version is not a substitute for reading *The Deal*, which is a book that, quite literally, can change or save your life. I include the shortened version here with the author's consent only because it is so vitally important. Doing "the Deal" may be one of the most important steps you ever take in life.

The Deal

1. Starting

It is very simple to do the Deal. You need a half-hour to an hour where you will be able to sit quietly, in private, without interruptions (including electronic pings). You can do it seated at your desk during a lunch hour, on a plane ride, or during a train commute, as long as you will not be disturbed. Have this text handy so that you can read the pertinent passages, follow the directions, and then continue.

2. Centering

Sit upright in a comfortable chair. Be relaxed but alert. Close your eyes and sense your body as it rests in the seat. Bring your attention to your breath. Take a couple of deep breaths to relax. Allow your breath to go easily in and out, and just watch the flow. Continue for about two minutes.

As you are doing this thoughts and images will appear in your mind. This is natural and expected. Allow them. Just relax and watch the thoughts, whatever they are. Also watch what emotions arise. Don't try to change anything—just observe.

At this point you are probably feeling somewhat relaxed. Return your attention to your breath. Focus on the center of your chest near your heart. See if you can make some kind of connection between the breath and this heart area. You may feel warmth or tightness in the chest, or some other sensation. Just let your attention rest there for a few seconds.

3. Releasing the Present

Now go to a "secret place" in your heart. Don't think about it or ask what it means—just allow this to happen. You will probably feel that you are in a quiet, still, and very private space that is all your own.

As you rest in the privacy of your own heart, look inwardly at things you think you've done wrong in the recent past—maybe you said something hurtful; broke your word; failed to make good on a debt or a payment in a timely way. Think also of whatever is currently troubling you. Maybe you have a problem with a neighbor; maybe you don't feel that you have enough money. Maybe you think some of this is your fault.

Then let your attention then to go to what you think of as your personal failings. You may think "I get angry too easily" or "I eat too much," or some such. Allow yourself to observe the images and emotions that may accompany these things.

Now, in this secret place in your heart, ask yourself, "*Do I want to be released from all these things?*" You are not asking *how* this will happen, but simply whether you want to be free from these burdens.

If your answer is *no*, ask yourself if this is because you believe it is impossible to be released in this way. But do not get lost in focusing right now on what you think is possible. You are merely deciding what you want. If your answer remains *no*, then bring this exercise to a close by returning your attention to the sensations of your body and allowing your eyes to open. There is nothing wrong in deciding not to go further with this process. It may simply mean that it is not for you, or that it's not the right time. *You can try it again at any time.*

If the answer to the above questions is *yes*, take a deep breath and release all of these oppressive thoughts and images.

4.   Releasing the Past

Now allow your mind to go further back in time perhaps to the last year or so. Think of the things you feel guilty for—saying something cruel, breaking a promise, cheating on a mate. You may feel guilty for small things, like missing an appointment or not returning a phone call. You may think of ways that you have hurt yourself, perhaps failing to stand up for yourself, or making what you consider a stupid mistake.

Ask again, *"Do I want to be released from all these things?"*

Now go back further, scanning back over the past several years of your life. You may think of things that you've failed to complete, people you've hurt, lies you've told, failure to stand up for a friend. Allow these offenses to surface. Take as much time as you want to look at these things. Again, emotions may come up; let them.

Allow this process to continue back to your earliest memories. There's no way that you can think of all the things you've done that you feel bad about—just make sure you aren't blocking anything.

Now ask again, *"Do I want to be released from all these things?"* You may hear something deep inside you say *"yes,"* or you may feel a sense of comfort or lightness. Take a deep breath and let it out.

At this point you can open your eyes for a moment or two if you like, or even get up and stretch and walk around the room for a minute. But stay nearby to where you were seated.

5.   Releasing Others

Sit down again. Let your eyes close, and let your attention return gently to your breath and bodily sensations.

Bring to mind someone toward whom you are angry, or against whom you are holding a grudge. Focus on one person. Picture this person as if he or she is standing before you.

Ask yourself now, *"Am I willing to forgive this person?"*

If the answer is *no*, just remember that you want to be released from many things yourself, and this is an essential part of that process. Ask yourself again, *"Am I willing to forgive this person?"*

If the answer remains *no*, then you can bring the exercise to a close, and gently open your eyes. Don't force it; you can always return to it.

If the answer is *yes*, allow your image of the person to fade from your mind.

Now let your attention go to all the grievances, grudges, and hostilities you are holding. This includes anyone you are angry with, such as coworkers, spouses or ex-spouses, parents, siblings, neighbors, friends, and, of course, enemies. Focus on those who are irritating you the most in your daily life right now.

Now ask yourself, *"Am I willing to forgive all of these people?"*

If the answer is *no*, ask yourself which person or persons you don't want to forgive. Remind yourself that your grievances do not harm this person; *you* are the only one they hurt. Then ask yourself again, *"Am I willing to forgive this person?"*

If the answer remains *no*, you can bring the exercise to a close for now and gently open your eyes.

If the answer is *yes*, allow the images of these people to fade in your mind.

Finally, let your attention go to your past, including all the people that you can think of who have ever hurt you. Again, you don't need to think of every last person. But let as many individuals as possible come to mind, and make sure not to consciously exclude anyone.

You can also let your mind go to the evils of the

world—warfare, killing, terrorism, cruelty, irresponsibility. Do not look for an answer to these things right now—there will be other times for that. Just allow your feelings and emotions to arise. Observe them, do not judge them, and then let them go.

Ask, "*Am I willing to forgive all these people and all these things?*"

If the answer is *no*, focus on the person or people against whom you still hold a grudge. Once more, no matter how much a person may have hurt you, your anger does no harm to him or her; it harms only you.

Ask again, "*Am I willing to forgive all these people?*"

If the answer remains *no*, then you can bring the exercise to a close for now, and gently open your eyes.

If it is *yes* let them fade from your mind for the time being.

6. Closing

Focus again on your body and your breath. Let your attention return to all the things for which you want to be forgiven. Picture the images and emotions associated with these—see them located in front of you to your left side.

As you look at these things, say to yourself, "*I ask to be forgiven for all these things.*" If you wish, you can also ask forgiveness from God.

Now let your attention focus on all the people you want to forgive. Picture them too as being located in front of you—to your right side.

Say to yourself, "*I forgive all of you for everything.*" You can also add, "*I ask God (or Jesus or a Higher Power) to forgive you for everything as well.*"

Now release all the images, thoughts, feelings, and people that you see in front of you. Let them fade from your mind. Allow yourself to feel free of all these burdens.

Say to yourself: *"It is done. I have forgiven everything and I accept forgiveness for everything."*

Congratulations. You have done the Deal: you forgive everything and are forgiven for everything. It is the law, and it works: *Your debts are forgiven as you have forgiven your debtors.*

7.   Taking Action

Keep your eyes closed for a final—and optional—step. Ask yourself if you need to make amends to anyone as part of this process. You do not need to resurrect the past or reinsert yourself or others into uncomfortable situations. If it will cause no harm or discomfort, however, is there anyone you need to speak to, to say that you forgive or ask forgiveness of? Do you need to make things right with anyone? This is entirely at your discretion. *You are not required to take any external action as a result of the Deal.*

Take a few deep breaths and relax before opening your eyes. If any powerful emotions have come up, allow yourself to feel them without any self-criticism. Gradually return to your ordinary state of consciousness; stand up when you are ready.

8.   Integrating

If a sink or source of clean water is available, you may want to wash your hands and face with the symbolic intention of cleansing yourself from the grievances and resentments of the past. If this is not possible right away, do it later. This action is not absolutely necessary, but it can help to perform a small ceremony to signal completion of the Deal.

You should honor what you have just done. Your actions this hour will have positive consequences beyond what you may expect. If you can, take some time by yourself. You might take a walk or rest a bit. Don't feel the need to tell anyone what you have done.

A word of caution: you may feel a sense of euphoria immediately after doing the Deal. You might feel the urge to take some radical step in your life. *It would be wise to pause for at least three days after doing the Deal.* Take time out before any "big" moves.

9. Reinforcing

Finally, you may want to reinforce what you have done with a daily spiritual practice of some kind. (Such a practice is recommended below.) A useful practice in maintaining the Deal is to simply send thoughts of love, peace, and blessing to everyone in the world. You can do this silently whenever you wish, at any time. You may also want to mentally send blessings to people in your home, at work, or out in public. You will not necessarily see any automatic results from this—but on occasions you may be surprised at what happens.

Now that you've done the Deal, to help sustain your sense of forgiveness I recommend a personal affirmation, which I first discovered in the work of Unity minister Catherine Ponder. When thinking of someone you need to forgive, or from whom you need to gain a healthy distance, fix a mental picture of the person and affirm, silently or aloud: "I bless you and release you to your highest good." Repeat this as many times as necessary, whenever necessary. This simple little manta has proven itself repeatedly in my experience. It can be used either to address past hurts, or resentments that come up in the moment.

Virtue Pays

If you are unmoved by the ideas in this chapter—if notions of the golden rule, the circle of ethics, and forgiveness leave you unconvinced—let me offer you one final concept: *Virtue pays.* Heed carefully the statement below from Objectivist philosopher Leonard Peikoff, a disciple of Ayn Rand. He offers a different—and compelling—view of virtue:

> Virtue is not automatically rewarded, but this does not change the fact that it *is* rewarded. Virtue minimizes the risks inherent in life and maximizes the chance of success. Morality teaches one how to gain and use the full power of one's mind, how to choose one's associates, how to organize society so that the best among men rise to the top. It teaches one how to safeguard life and limb in principle and therefore against every danger that can be foreseen. This does not give men omnipotence; what it gives them is the means of preventing, mitigating, or counteracting innumerable evils that would otherwise be intractable.

An outstanding book on how virtue pays has the unlikely title *How to Attract Good Luck*. It may sound like a gambling guide, but it is the furthest thing from it. Economist, journalist, and diplomat A.H.Z. Carr wrote the book in 1952. Carr had served as an economic advisor in the presidential administrations of Franklin Roosevelt and Harry Truman, and also spent time on economic and diplomatic missions in Europe and the Far East. He amassed a great deal of experience in observing ambitious people, and how careers in diplomacy and business were made—and broken.

In *How to Attract Good Luck* Carr demonstrated how many of our personal reversals and failings result from impetuous, shortsighted, or unethical behavior. Such qualities deter good luck, and their opposites invite it. By "luck" Carr meant not blind chance but rather certain patterns of behavior that bend circumstances to our favor. Here I digest some of Carr's insights on how *virtue pays*:

- Demonstrate "unexpected friendliness" to colleagues, strangers, or casual acquaintances. In the history of religion and myth, displays of unwarranted hospitality or friendliness often prove the turning point where rewards are showered on someone who unknowingly aids an angel or the gods.
- Pursue topics or lines of work for which you feel *zest*. This is a recipe for fortuitous connections and relationships.
- Boredom is a harbinger of bad luck. Boredom leads you to rash or frivolous actions in pursuit of relief. Stay busy and engaged.

- Generosity is almost always rewarded.
- Watch for "small chances" to accomplish your aims. A small step, either in conjunction with other small steps or by itself, can produce unexpected results.
- Stay alert for larger "critical chances"—always be watchful.
- "It is lucky to know what we want." Focus brings us right action.
- Never imagine yourself more formidable or skilled than you really are. Be realistic about your current level of abilities and where they must grow.
- Healthful self-respect keeps you out of trouble.
- Avoid hyper-competitive colleagues and acquaintances. "Those who make us feel competitive," Carr wrote, "easily can tempt us into unlucky displays of egotism."
- Always look for ways to turn chance events into good use.
- William James: "A single successful effort of moral volition, such as saying 'no' to some habitual temptation, or performing some courageous act, will launch a man on a higher level of energy for days or weeks, will give him a new range of power."
- Prejudice brings bad luck.
- Ethical courage, not impulsiveness or truculence, imbues you with nobility. Defending a loved person or cause is almost always a lucky act.
- Acting without integrity invites misfortune.
- Envy moves you to foolish actions and petty thoughts. It brings bad luck.
- Carr: "Any effort we make, however slight, to prevent the dictation of our behavior by insecurity feelings is a step toward luckiness."

ACTION STEP:
Close Each Day This Way

Napoleon Hill wrote the following prayer, which he recommended saying at the end of each day. If praying is not for you, then recite it as a statement of personal ethics, altering the language to suit your heart. *"I ask not for more blessings, but more wisdom with which to make better use of the blessings I now possess. And give me, please, more understanding that I may occupy more space in the hearts of my fellow men by rendering more service tomorrow than I have rendered today."*

TAKEAWAY POINTS:

- The Golden Rule holds more truth and power than you imagine. Use it to govern not only your actions but also your thoughts. It is the greatest personal tool we possess.

- Take care that your aim and your actions form a "Circle of Ethics" in which everyone involved benefits.

- Enduring success arises from filling a genuine human need.

- Strive to be independent, non-conformist, and self-directed. Narrow ambition and herd thinking lead nowhere.

- The right aim is accompanied by a distinctive fearlessness.

- *Avoid gossip*—always and everywhere. It poisons all involved. This is the simplest and greatest improvement you can make to your life. Do it now.

- You are what you think and do. There is no "inner" and "outer," no "business" and "personal"—it's all *one life*.

- Forgiveness is not some namby-pamby virtue; it can unlock tremendous possibilities in your life.

- Do "The Deal"—it takes one hour and it can change everything. You will feel and act more free after.

- Good ethics bring you returns beyond what you may imagine. *Virtue pays*.

4

Refining Your Aim

We now get down to the fine points of writing down your aim, revising it, and incorporating money into your vision and planning

First off, writing down your aim is incredibly important. *Never neglect this step.* A written goal has special power. This seemingly small act represents the inceptive actualization of your aim in the world. Like a marriage certificate, a contract, or a legal statute, the power of the written word carries the weight of commitment.

It is natural and expected that you may need to revise your aim for some time before it rings exactly right to you. You may finally feel that you have nailed it, only to reverse yourself. This is all part of the process. The objective is to keep at it until you arrive at a short, vivid statement of absolute integrity.

I am writing these words just before the July 4th holiday. When America's founders declared independence from the British crown they didn't just *say* what they intended to do. What attention would that have gotten? They wrote the Declaration of Independence (the primary text was written by Thomas Jefferson), and delegates at the state house in Philadelphia individually signed it. There was definiteness of commitment in that—and physical risk. Why should you be any less serious in devising your chief aim? This is your life. Take it seriously.

Sharpening Your DCA

You are, in a sense, staking your life on your DCA. This is why I keep emphasizing the need to devise your statement with care. I want to share with you the refining process of my friend Tim Botta, an artist whose portrait of Napoleon Hill can be found at the front of the print and digital editions of this book. As of this writing, Tim's DCA is to transition from being a semi-professional to a professional artist. Here is his first DCA combined with a plan of action. It is followed by a revised and improved version.

My definite major purpose is to be a professional artist and illustrator, making a living at art. I will concentrate on ink drawings on paper, acrylic paintings, and digital art. I will provide versatile illustrations for books, magazines, and websites. My illustrations will mostly be imaginative portraits. To promote my professional work, and to provide samples for art directors, I will create an online portfolio of illustrations to which to refer art directors. I will also contact art directors with samples of my illustrations. My paintings will be sold online and through galleries that specialize in representational art.

By January 1, 2017, I will earn enough be able to transition from semi-professional to professional and meet all my financial obligations, and independently provide myself and my cat with health insurance. By January 1, 2021, I will earn at least $100,000 per year and have at least one million dollars in savings and investments and be debt-free. In exchange for this pay, I intend to render service in the capacity of an artist and illustrator, creating beautiful, emotional, and popular works of art that reveal the essence of their subject and promote a positive spirit in the world (as the Beatles did). My artwork will also portray the consciousness of a free person (for example, members of Jefferson Airplane, or David Ossman and other members of the Firesign Theatre). I will create works of outstanding quality and in such a quantity that I will be known as highly productive and prolific as an artist. The money that I earn will be used to fund my art, as well as vastly improve the quality of life for myself and all loved ones (including of course my cat—and any other cats I may rescue and adopt—and Lynda's cats). I also will use a percentage of the money I earn to promote and support animal rescue and animal protection. Any recognition I get for my art I will also use as a platform to promote and support animal rescue and animal protection. I also will continue to promote the ideas and values of the positive-thinking movement through visual art.

My plan is to create interest in my artwork through social and other media, and by creating instructional videos and instructional articles for artists' magazines and online, and to earn money by creating illustrations for books, magazines, and other media, as well as selling original works both online and in galleries.

I will synthesize various styles from illustration art and fine art into a new and exciting style that people will enjoy.

As a legacy, my artwork will appear in galleries and books. Also as part of my legacy, I will bestow gifts on animal rescue and protection organizations, and also use the money I have earned to endow a foundation for animal rescue and protection.

When I read Tim's statement, I found it strong—and I made the following comments:

1. In your opening line, be more specific about precisely what forms and media your artwork will take.

2. Relating to that point, have you created or are you creating organized plans to carry out this professional work? Have you researched the venues and customers, and their needs?

3. I think your dates are sound but I would say "I will" rather than "I would like to"—which also means feeling certain about the two points above.

4. Use present tense more; you are doing some of this work already.

5. Focus your efforts. Some of what's here—books, instructional videos, magazines—sound very different to me.

After some back and forth, Tim produced a more precise revision, which is below. It is idealistic, ambitious, and realistic. It sets clear aims, and outlines some of the vehicles he is using to get there.

> I am a professional artist and illustrator, making a good living at art. I concentrate on ink drawings on paper, acrylic paintings, and digital art. I provide versatile illustrations for books, magazines, and websites, primarily those in the areas of self-help and motivation. My illustrations are chiefly imaginative portraits of historical figures from the positive-thinking movement
>
> To promote my professional work I am creating a beautiful online portfolio of illustrations. I am contacting at least one art director per week with samples of my illustrations.
>
> By January 1, 2017, I earn at least $30,000 per year, making me able to transition from semi-professional to professional and meet all my financial obligations and independently

provide myself and my cat with health insurance. By January 1, 2021, I earn at least $100,000 per year and have at least one million dollars in savings and investments and am debt-free. In exchange for this, I provide service as an artist and illustrator, creating beautiful, emotional, and popular works of art that reveal the essence of their subject and promote a positive spirit in the world (as the Beatles did). My artwork embodies the consciousness of a free person (for example, members of Jefferson Airplane, or David Ossman and other members of the Firesign Theatre). I create works of outstanding quality and in such a quantity that I am known as a highly productive and prolific artist. My earnings fund my art, as well as vastly improve the quality of life for myself and all my loved ones (including of course my cat—and any other cats I may rescue and adopt—and Lynda's cats). I also use a percentage of the money I earn to promote and support animal rescue and animal protection. I use my recognition as an artist to promote and support animal rescue and animal protection. I also promote the ideas and values of the positive-thinking movement through visual art.

I am acting on my organized plan to concentrate on creating imaginative and inspiring portraits of New Thought heroes for an audience of self-help and motivational readers. I provide merchandise (including prints, T-shirts, and other items like coffee mugs) through my Café

Press shop. My artwork is a part of my audience's everyday life, giving them inspiration and encouragement.

I synthesize various styles from illustration art and fine art into a new and exciting style that people enjoy.

As a legacy, my artwork will appear in galleries and books. Also as part of my legacy, I will bestow gifts on animal rescue and protection organizations, and also use the money I have earned to endow a foundation for animal rescue and protection.

"So Be It! See To It!"

Few people, in any field, have written a more compelling statement of aims than bestselling science-fiction author Octavia Butler (1947-2006), who we first met in chapter one.

Growing up a gangly, lonely African-American kid in Pasadena in the 1950s and 60s, Butler determined early on to become a novelist. Just as she began to breakthrough as a writer, Butler handwrote the following mission statement in 1988 in one of her notebooks. The pioneering writer crafted one of the most prescient, specific, and value-driven statements of purpose that I have ever seen. Study it and learn from it.

I shall be a bestselling writer.

After *Imago*, each of my books will be on the bestseller lists of LAT, NYT, PW, WP, etc.

My novels will go onto the above lists <u>whether publishers push them hard or not</u>, whether I'm paid a high advance or not.

This is my life. I write bestselling novels. My novels go onto the bestseller lists on or shortly after publication. My novels <u>each</u> travel <u>up</u> to the <u>top</u> and they <u>stay on top</u> for months (at least two). Each of my novels does this.

<u>So be it!</u>

<u>See to it!</u>

I will find the way to do this. So be it! See to it!

My books will be read by millions of people!

I will buy a beautiful home in an excellent neighborhood.

I will send poor black youngsters to Clarion or other writer's workshops.

I will help poor black youngsters broaden their horizons.

I will help poor black youngsters go to college.

I will get the best of health care for my mother and myself.

I will hire a car whenever I want or need to.

I will travel whenever and wherever in the world that I choose.

My books will be <u>read</u> by <u>millions of people</u>!

So be it! See to it!

Reread Butler's statement. Rewrite it by hand. Memorize it. Let its power permeate your psyche. And always remember: Butler invested every word of her statement with labor, study, and personal trial. Her statement is powerful precisely because she backed it with constant effort and enormous authorial talent. Also note that her statement, and Tim's above it, capture the zeal and specificity required to attain *any* worthy goal, whether starting a business, attaining distinction in your profession, or completing a heartfelt personal project. The ingredients of success, whatever your focus, are remarkably similar.

Your Daily Commitment

I am now going to supply you with an extremely powerful exercise adapted from *Think and Grow Rich*. This exercise is at the heart of my personal daily practice. First, I want you to write out your Definite Chief Aim in a new document. Next I want you to list how much money you intend to earn from your DCA and by what date. E.g., "I earn a yearly salary of $150,000 from all sources by [month/year]." Add what service or product you will deliver for the money. E.g., "I earn this sum through my work as a home-organizer, which frees up my clients to spend more time on their work and with their families." Be definite. (And if you find it difficult to attach a dollar amount to your DCA don't worry—I deal more fully with this question later in this chapter.)

Below your DCA and statement of earnings, write out or copy the five-steps below, just as they appear here. (You've encountered step five earlier, which I advised posting where you can see it for constant reference.) Once you've done all that print the document and sign your name to it. Or, if you prefer, add your signature digitally and save it on your device or laptop, wherever it is most accessible. Read the statement with full feeling at least once each day. (Napoleon Hill recommended once but at first you can also try doing it once in the morning and again in the evening.) This same passage was found handwritten—and signed—in the journals of martial artist and movie actor Bruce Lee.

First. I know that I have the ability to achieve the object of my DEFINITE PURPOSE in life, therefore, I demand of myself persistent, continuous action toward its attainment, and I here and now promise to render such action.

Second. I realize the dominating thoughts of my mind will eventually reproduce themselves in outward physical action, and gradually transform themselves into physical reality. Therefore, I will concentrate my thoughts for thirty minutes daily upon the task of thinking of the person I intend to become, thereby creating in my mind a clear mental picture of that person.

Third. I know that through the principle of autosuggestion any desire that I persistently hold in my mind will eventually seek expression through some practical means of attaining the object back of it. Therefore, I will devote ten minutes daily to demanding of myself the development of self-confidence.

Fourth. I have clearly written down a description of my DEFINITE CHIEF AIM in life, and I will never stop trying until I have developed sufficient self-confidence for its attainment.

Fifth. I fully realize that no wealth or position can long endure unless built upon truth and justice. Therefore, I will engage in no transaction that does not benefit all whom it affects. I will succeed by attracting to myself the forces I wish to use, and the cooperation of other people. I will induce others to serve me, because of my willingness to serve others. I will eliminate hatred, envy, jealousy, selfishness, and cynicism, by developing love for all humanity, because I know that a negative attitude toward others can never bring me success. I will cause others to believe in me because I will believe in them, and in myself.

I will sign my name to this formula, commit it to memory, and repeat it aloud once [or twice] a day, with full FAITH that it will gradually influence my THOUGHTS and ACTIONS, so that I will become a self-reliant and successful person.

How Ideas Work

Ideas take you only part of the way home. We often hear that one good idea can change your life. That sounds nice, but it isn't exactly right. There is another ingredient necessary: A great idea, in order to really mean something, must be brilliantly executed. Inertia, arising from lack of know-how, procrastination (which is really fear), or an absence of talent, dooms most great ideas. Most ideas amount to no more than idle talk.

"There are a lot of great ideas out there," a billionaire investor once told me. "But great execution is a lot rarer than great ideas. When I invest, I look for great execution more than great ideas."

The social philosopher Michael Walzer said something related: "An idea must have a constituency," or it is of no significance. Whatever the nature of your aim or idea, if you lack ability to carry it out, or communicate it, it withers.

Great execution begins with *specialized knowledge.* Napoleon Hill put it this way:

> "KNOWLEDGE will not attract money unless it is organized, and intelligently directed through practical PLANS OF ACTION . . . Lack of understanding of this fact has been the source of confusion to millions who people who falsely believe that 'knowledge is power.' It is nothing of the sort! Knowledge is only *potential* power."

There are, Hill noted, two kinds of knowledge: general knowledge and specialized knowledge. General knowledge is virtually worthless: it accomplishes little and often gets you nowhere, unless you enjoy playing trivia nights at your local bar. The key, Hill noted, is to seek and apply *specialized knowledge.*

To acquire *specialized knowledge*, you must distinguish among which sources to trust—you must ensure that the information you are getting is accurate, relevant, and up to date. First, you must separate facts from mere information. Much "information" is not based upon facts but upon rumor, opinion, and casually tossed-off judgments. Second, you must divide *facts* into two classes: *important* and *unimportant.* All facts that *aid* your pursuit of your DCA (without violating the rights of others) are *important* and *relevant*. Facts that you cannot use are the opposite. If you direct your attention exclusively to the *important facts*—those that contribute to the realization of your aim—you will attain specialized and accurate knowledge, and along with it a special clarity and focus.

This is part of why I have stressed avoiding gossip, neither spreading nor listening to it. If you permit yourself to be swayed by sundry information—especially rumors and gossip—you will never become an *accurate thinker*, and you will not attain your definite chief aim. Idle chatter, tale bearing, rumors, casual opinion, and superfluous information—these must be shunned.

The Formula

I noted above that most ideas die for lack of good execution. Ralph Waldo Emerson lamented this truth: "But the idea and execution are not often intrusted to the same head. There is some incompatibility of good speculation and practice, for example, the failure of monasteries and Brook Farms. To hammer out phalanxes must be done by smiths; as soon as the scholar attempts it, he is half a charlatan."

Napoleon Hill hinted at an action formula for great execution. I have taken what he implied and mapped it out here. This formula allows you to understand the necessary factors in combining ideas with specialized knowledge to produce a successful combination. Hill referenced elements of this formula throughout his chapter on "Specialized Knowledge" in *Think and Grow Rich*. I have taken those elements and put them into an equation, which will help you put them into action. Here it is:

IMAGINATION + ORGANIZED PLANS
connects
SPECIALIZED KNOWLEDGE with IDEAS

Look at the words I've capitalized above. None of those factors *alone* amount to anything. Imagination without a plan is fantasy; a plan without imagination is listlessness; knowledge without an idea is inertia; an idea without knowledge is speculation. But this special combination forms a mental alchemy that brings focus and action to your DCA.

Put differently, IMAGINATION, taking the form of ORGANIZED PLANS (not daydreams), connects IDEAS to SPECIALIZED KNOWLEDGE. Let's say you have an idea: you want to run a mobile pet-grooming service. How do you make it work? How do you reach people? What kind of truck or vehicle do you need? Is your grooming ability up to par? Etc. Using your IMAGINATION to map out the scenario, and everything you need to get done (expressed as ORGANIZED PLANS), allows you to bridge the gap between your IDEA and the SPECIALIZED KNOWLEDGE required to get your operation off the ground. You may need the help of others to attain some of this SPECIALIZED KNOWLEDGE. You may have to pay for it. You almost certainly need to do extensive research.

All of these faculties of your mind—IMAGINATION + ORGANIZED PLANS connecting

SPECIALIZED KNOWLEDGE with IDEAS—combine to build the bridge from thought to action, and hence bring focus and possibility to your DCA.

Who Are You Listening To?

When you are researching and refining your DCA, and especially when you are seeking *specialized knowledge*, you must avoid the opinions of people who have no understanding of your field. This is especially true of friends and relatives who are often brimming over with opinions that they are only too eager to splatter all over your dreams. Who are *they* to judge you as an entrepreneur, teacher, artist, or investor? Have *they* distinguished themselves in your field of choice—*or in any field*?

"*Without doubt, the most common weakness of all human beings,*" Napoleon Hill wrote, "*is the habit of leaving their minds open to the negative influence of other people.* This weakness is all the more damaging, because most people do not recognize they are cursed by it, and many who acknowledge it, neglect or refuse to correct the evil until it becomes an uncontrollable part of their daily habits."

Do you recall step three of the Three-Step Miracle? It is silence. The only people you should speak to about what you are doing are those who have specialized knowledge of your field and the willingness to share or fairly sell knowledge. The one exception to this is members of your Master Mind alliance, a topic we'll explore in the next chapter.

Be wary even of "experts." Brilliant or accomplished people are simply wrong from time to time. Remember that. Let me tell you a story about when an expert wrongly advised me. In my work as a publisher I have been particularly successful in reissuing public-domain works—that is, works that have fallen out of copyright for reasons of expiration or non-renewal. This specialized field has been profitable and personally rewarding for me. It has allowed me to expose new generations of readers to some of the "golden oldies" of self-help that touch my heart, and it has been remunerative.

When I was a young editor contemplating the possibilities of public-domain publishing, I attended a 1998 conference on copyrights and public-domain law. Under intense corporate lobbying, Congress had passed legislation that year extending general copyright terms from 75 to 95 years. It was clear that Congress was intent on limiting, if not eliminating, the public-domain category entirely.

I approached one of the panelists, an observant and accomplished expert in rights management. I spoke to her about my interests and she quickly picked up on what I was driving at. She said: "Look, if you're thinking about creating a public-domain publishing program, forget it. Congress is just going to keep narrowing what enters the public domain. There's no future there."

She was wrong. What she did not understand was that a huge and overlooked swath of highly desirable books on positive-mind and motivational spirituality—my area of specialty—had quietly fallen into public domain because of previous wrinkles in copyright law. Mind you, I didn't fully know this at the time. It was a hunch, which I worked hard to successfully confirm. I did extensive research, learning the ins and outs of copyright law, and determining the various circum-stances under which books enter public domain. As it happened, many books that were published during a renaissance in American motivational literature were now public domain, regardless of what Congress did. This material keenly interested me, both personally and professionally.

Simultaneously, other people, both friends and a few business acquaintances, were also telling me that public-domain publishing was dead. They argued that new technologies, such as on-demand printing, eBooks, and digital databases, would mean that every-thing worth reading would be automatically available, either for free or at a very low price, and there would be no market for public-domain reissues. The nay-sayers were all wrong. I quietly discovered that not only had a great deal of commercially appealing liter-ature fallen through the cracks of those technologies (technology doesn't curate—people do), but also that self-help readers like me were very willing to buy well-produced, handsome editions of classic works. Being able to download a free book on your phone—if you really intend to read it and live by it—doesn't pre-clude or replace owning a quality edition. Readers of self-help like to fold pages, make notes, highlight, and underline—and for that you need (and ought to have) your own tactile copy. Plus, when you treasure a book you like having a well-produced edition, perhaps newly typeset, with a dignified cover and good packaging. As a self-help reader, I want all these things. I knew others would, too. And even in digital editions, good produc-tion values still matter.

When told of my plans to produce quality reissue editions, one (slightly cynical) financier told me: "Oh, I get it: it's like selling water in designer bottles. It's the same water in a fancy container." No, it is not like that at all. A lover of self-help respects his or her favorite works; people who read *Alcoholics Anonymous*, for example, attach almost Scriptural significance to that great work. Not just any edition will do. It's not about old water in new bottles. It is about making the book public in a way that honors its worth and provides a well-produced edition for posterity and study.

I had an instinct for all of this because, unlike most of those who sought to give me advice, I was, and remain, an avid reader of self-help. I put my instincts to the test through research, experience, and action—I explored what was available, what sold, what worked, what didn't, and where the valuable works were. I read huge numbers of them. I had success from the moment I began reissuing self-development classics in 2005, and never looked back (or ran out of quality works).

Our instincts are not always right; we must gather data to back them up. But never let anyone, especially someone from outside your field, tell you about your business, profession, or art. Be careful, too, of what you read online. The digital world is flooded with indiscriminate information. As noted earlier, scrutinize your sources and ask: Is this person, course, or publication something that warrants my trust? Accept nothing at face value.

Also, use numbers—gather piles of them. So many that you throw out 90% of what you've found. What are you selling, making, or buying? How much does it cost? Who is the consumer? What does he or she earn? How frequent are their purchases? What is the competition? You can find data online, in libraries, through good textbooks and courses, and through in-person visits to people, facilities, offices, and shops that are willing to open their doors to you. Never underestimate the value of face-to-face visits to people and places that are relevant to your DCA. People like the opportunity to display what they know—but make sure that the person doing the talking has accurate and current information.

And, finally, never accept someone else's judgment as the final word on anything. Verify, verify, verify. The billionaire investor who told me about the importance of "great execution" shared another story. When he was younger he was opening an office for one of his firms in a Midwestern city that had been hit hard by an economic slump. Stores along main street were boarded up and parts of town looked abandoned. "It was terrible," he recalled.

He met with a local landlord about renting office space. The man took him to the space, rolled out the floor plan to show him the square footage, and was blunt about the rent: he told him his monthly mortgage and explained that he was charging rent that covered his costs, and nothing more. "You won't get a better deal anywhere," the landlord said. My acquaintance replied: "I don't know that. Maybe the guy across the street is even more under water than you and will give me his space at half the mortgage."

He was not telling the story as a lesson in ruthlessness. He was demonstrating that no matter how obvious the facts may appear, and no matter how authoritative or straight talking someone may seem, always, *always* check things out for yourself.

Another investor calls it seeking "out-of-box information." He makes a practice of *not* reading the financial trades, reports to stockholders and investors, or data provided by companies or people seeking venture capital. Rather, he goes around those sources and researches things for himself, such as hiring an engineer to gather his own core sample from an oil field. This investor is always seeking independent, verifiable data so as not to rely on someone else's spin.

"Fortunes are made," he said, "on out-of-box information."

Quality Rules

People of a certain generation were once wary of "selling out." Or becoming "part of the system." Although these terms are no longer widely heard today, they reflect a healthy concern. But this concern is not *strictly necessary*. There is a simple definition of selling out. It means: *putting money before quality*. That's all. If you can truly stand by the efficacy and integrity of your service, art, or product, then no sum of money or act of salesmanship should ever make you feel that you are selling out.

What's more, there exist certain compromises that are artistically and commercially valid. I know a film director who was editing one of his movies under the gun of a deadline by which the film had to be enrolled in a film festival. He and his backers needed to be part of the festival for the film's exposure and distribution. Without feeling that he was entirely finished with his editing, he let the film go because failing to do so would have spelled financial disaster, and it would have meant breaking his word to his backers and others. His commitment mattered as much as his drive for perfection. He did not compromise the essential vision or outlook of his project. But he let it go to the festival—and did the right thing.

The musician Frank Zappa, a figure of artistic integrity, appeared one night on the David Letterman Show. Zappa was promoting a new album on which the London Symphony Orchestra played symphonic versions of his compositions. In what I thought was a remarkable display of bluntness, the composer volunteered to Letterman that the album did not sound exactly like it was supposed to. Zappa explained that it was extremely expensive to book rehearsal time with the London Symphony, and he didn't have the money to cover as many rehearsals as he would have liked. He had already agreed to a budget, he had backers, and he had a commitment. Zappa did his artistic best with what was available, kept his commitment, and released the album.

My wish is that every work of art and product is produced to total perfection. Steve Jobs was a master at that. But there are honest compromises, such as those above. They are valid. So long as a product is safe, of quality, and clearly marketed, labeled, and sold, so long as you do not skew or gut its essentials, you are not "selling out." You are honoring your commitments and keeping your word.

Money Matters

Money is a vital part of success and is necessary to sustain any kind of project. You will not feel successful unless you are properly remunerated. You may want far more than good pay—you may want riches. That is a sound and healthy aim. In *Think and Grow Rich*, Napoleon Hill devised a formula for financial success (he did call it *Think and Grow Rich*, after all). I have adapted his formula below. Follow each step with great care. This exercise should be approached with the solemnity of a life contract, which is exactly what it is.

First. Fix in your mind the *exact* amount of money you desire. It is not sufficient merely to say, "I want plenty of money." Be definite as to the amount.

Second. Determine exactly what service or product you intend to provide in return for the money you desire.

Third. Establish a definite date when you intend to *possess* the money you desire.

Fourth. Create *a definite plan* for carrying out your desire, and begin *at once*, whether or not you are ready, to put this plan into *action*.

Fifth. Write out a clear, concise statement of the amount of money you intend to acquire, name the time limit for its acquisition, state what you intend to give in return for the money, and describe clearly the plan through which you intend to accumulate it.

Sixth. Read your written statement aloud, twice daily, once just before retiring at night and once after arising in the morning. *As you read—see and feel and believe yourself already in possession of the money.*

It is especially important, Hill taught, that you observe and follow step six. You may feel that is impossible to "see yourself in possession of money" before you actually have it. Here is where a *burning desire* comes to your aid. If you truly desire money or another goal, and feel it so deeply that your desire is an obsession, you will be able to convince yourself that it is in reach. This is another use of autosuggestion; it helps to orient your mind and attention toward your goal and, hence, to grow more keenly sensitive to opportunities to attain your objective. Remember that your goal must also be within the realm of possibility, as discussed in chapter two.

Choose Wealth

Money was vital and critically important in Napoleon Hill's worldview, as it should be in yours. As I mentioned, no project or undertaking can be experienced as a success unless it is financial viable. At the same time Hill wrote *Think and Grow Rich* and all of his success philosophy so that it can be applied in pursuit of any worthy aim. If your aim is not chiefly money, feel free to reorient the focus that you find above.

Some people feel conflicted about attaching money to their dreams—and for thoughtful reasons. In 2016 I heard from Kimberly:

I write children's books (I keep them happily in my drawer, however I have been encouraged by friends and some voice in myself to try to get them published). I am trying to use the books you recommend like Napoleon Hill's and *It Works*. I would love to have money . . . but at this point I just want to focus on getting one of the books published. Can I use Hill's ideas and just substitute the book instead of money? Or *It Works*? It seems there is overlap with the ideas or books you recommend . . . I am just trying to streamline my process.

I would love your opinion as to which pro-cess would work the best. The money part blocks my process because I have no idea what type of money to assign to my books (they were given to me by the wind and the standing stones at Avebury . . . and the wind did not assign a monetary value :)).

I told Kimberly that she should follow her heart and omit mention of money for the time being. But do not neglect money for the long run. If you are building schools for the poor, you require money to open and sustain them. If you are an artist, you need money for yourself and your loved ones. Again, I have learned from decades of experience in the world of publishing and elsewhere: No one feels truly good about a project unless it is finan-cially successfully, or at least viable, whatever the work's other merits. Resources are a natural part of life. Money serves as a means to goods, services, medicine, culture, education, and the fulfillment of critical needs. Money is a means of reward and recognition, both for your work and the work you require from others. At root, money is a relationship. It is not meant to rule your life. But it is a vital exchange.

Money also allows you to honor your vision. People of a certain generation remember the classic TV sit-com *The Monkees* (young people work with me . . .) about the hijinks of a Beatles-style sixties rock band. The "group" was made up of actors selected for their looks and comedic abilities. In real life producers would send them into the recording studio to lay down vocal tracks on top of songs written by others and recorded by studio musicians. As it happened, the members of The Monkees actually were real musicians and songwriters, and they wanted to play and write their own music. Ordinarily their producers would have laughed at the group's ambitions and told them to get back on set—but for one thing: In 1967 The Monkees sold many millions of records. That gave these artists commercial clout, which they used to demand that they be given a greater role in writing and selecting their own material, as well as playing instruments in studio and on stage. Although critics never quite warmed to the group (something that is changing today), The Monkees demonstrated that they were a *real* band after all. They never would have gotten that chance if they didn't have the force of the dollar behind them.

When I first started reading *Think and Grow Rich* I, too, was uncomfortable writing down a particular amount. I hesitated doing so. It felt unnatural. It seemed to me like I was closing off options or cheapening my priorities. Writing down a sum chaffed against my religious leanings. But I must tell you that once I got past those hesitancies, I found it extremely potent to commit to a definite figure and date.

As I am writing these words I am looking at a yellow sticky note pasted inside the back cover of my personal copy of *Think and Grow Rich* (whose jacket and spine I have covered in clear packing tape to keep the book from falling apart after multiple readings). My yellow note is dated 11/23/14 and lists a specific dollar amount, to which I committed to earning by the following year on 11/23/15 (which also happens to be my birthday). I later wrote an addendum on this piece of paper: "This happened!! 5/27/16." The latter date is when I had noticed, quite by surprise, that the sum I had written down arrived within the given timeframe.

Why did this happen? As I noted earlier, writing down and committing to a precise amount and deadline produce a unique pull on the mind, both consciously and, I suspect, subconsciously. When you orient yourself toward a concrete goal, you start to notice opportunities, people, possibilities, and ideas that can serve your objective. Accept my advice as that of a friend who wishes for your success: Do these exercises with exactitude.

Money Worries

In 2016 I heard from Jason in Washington, D.C., who emailed me to say that he was having difficulty figuring out how to make it financially practical to take his aim into the world. How, he asked, could he transition from his workaday job to his dream job as a movie producer while supporting a family?

"I'm having some difficulty transitioning the theory from the books into my life on a consistent basis," he explained, continuing:

> A little about me, I'm 41 and have always felt the desire to become a movie producer. However I exist in an environment where that idea seems intangible and I have trouble staying self motivated enough to bring my aspiration into fruition on my own. So I thought I would seek out some advice. I think one huge hindrance I have is that it seems as if I have to risk so much in order to pursue this goal. I understand that much of my hesitation is perceptual. However there is the reality that I have the responsibility of taking care of my family too.

I hear a lot of people voicing that question: How can I pursue what I love with so many current financial responsibilities? Before responding to his question I wanted to learn more. I asked him whether he is in proximity to the movie business or has a background in it. He replied:

> Well besides an internal affirmation that I should be a producer, I have not had much formal exposure to the industry. I've taken relevant course work in screenwriting and film studies in the past but nothing like an extensive curriculum leading to a degree in movie producing. I live in Washington, D.C., at the moment, which has limited opportunities to gain exposure to the

industry. I don't have formal a background in film producing but I've always been captivated by the drama of cinema. I believe I can be successful if I could step out of the current confinement of my thinking. Also I believe I was put on this earth to have more purpose and relevance than what I currently have. I'm moderately successful by external standards but internally I feel very mediocre. I just don't want to waste the remainder of my life drowned in mediocrity.

I was moved by Jason's words. I've been in that place myself—and I venture that anyone who wishes to expand his sense of possibility wrestles with the question of money. I responded to Jason as honestly as I could:

Thank you for expanding on that. Almost twenty years ago I felt much the same. I had been fired from a job at a political publisher (supposedly my dream job) and took a job at a New Age press that most of my friends and former colleagues regarded as slightly more prestigious than driving a Mister Softee truck. One author with whom I had previously worked closely, and regarded as a good friend, didn't even invite me to a holiday barbeque at his house. I had been active with a foreign book fair and the American organizers forgot all about me. I was like a nonentity to my former literary friends. I also felt a sense of lacking purpose: I was publishing books at random and not writing. Then in summer of 2003 the editors of *Science of Mind* asked me to interview baseball pitcher Barry Zito. [You'll recall this story from my introduction.] They had landed an interview with Barry (who uses mind metaphysics methods) and, frankly, they didn't want anyone who would embarrass them or screw it up. I wrote the piece and it totally reignited my passion for writing—and it gave me a sense of direction: writing about metaphysics. From there I built upwards, starting with some very small magazines. I think something that helped me was the capacity to just put pen to paper, so to speak, and begin writing. I didn't have to wait for anyone's green lights, although I certainly wanted them.

I think one of the core principles of achievement is beginning—right away, no matter on what level. Now, is producing exactly what you want? To my knowledge a producer financially backs movies and movie treatments, whether through his own money or, more often, an assemblage of investors. He selects, critiques, suggests, matches up talent, but, ultimately, he is a backer. If you have a passion for screenwriting, or for writing critically about cinema, that is something you could commence immediately (alongside your day job). Or, if producing really *is* your passion, I would start attending festivals, meeting filmmakers, checking out all channels of indie filmmaking to see who is there, what they're working on, and think about ideas that would allow you to take their projects to broader exposure. I know it's an overused expression but: think out of the box. Cinema is a huge and sprawling culture in America, from student documentaries to indie shorts to *Mad Max*. Where can you enter this world that would do good? What is missing from it?

If you are able, visit the Museum of the Moving Image here in New York (in Astoria, Queens—where there is a vibrant studio presence). Treat it like a religious pilgrimage. Walk the exhibit halls and get a sense of the roots and growth of this field that you love. If you are inclined toward religion (as I am) pray for guidance. Write down your goal—be very specific and clear. Then return to *Think and Grow Rich* and—my mantra—do the exercises from start to finish as if your life depends on it.

I then commented on the money question—and I want you to pay careful attention to this:

We often allow our plans to be stillborn by stopping and getting hung up on the question of how to earn a living doing what we love. But it is very important to separate those two needs for the time being. Making a living is an ever-present concern, and many great artists and inventors have kept their day jobs while pursuing their passions. What is absolutely vital is to BEGIN. If we equate these two things—earning a living and pursuing meaning—we may never begin. Let those two things be regarded separately for now.

I must underscore the importance of this point. Beginning means beginning. If you wait until the money comes into the picture it will ensure that your dream never even becomes a matter of experiment. Financial manager Michael Phillips put it this way in his insightful book *The Seven Laws of Money*: "Often people say to me 'What am I going to do next month? How am I to live until I get this thing started?' What I try to tell them is to get started; go forward; get something done. You have to worry about money for the next month as your own personal problem, in any case. Try to separate the issue of the project you're working on from your own problem of survival. If you're going to predicate the project's survival on your own need to be comfortable for the coming month, you have already doomed the project."

Philips does not advise jumping off a financial cliff. "Figure out how you're personally going to survive," he wrote, "and then, separately, how important the project is to you. You're going to have to continue to support yourself anyway, and when you're working on the project that's an added burden. But the project, per se, the success of the project, per se, will be seriously jeopardized if you integrate your own need to make a living with the needs of the project."

The task of getting by while you are building your project is one that you, and all of us, must work out individually; but never conflate your search for self-expression with the money needs of your life. If you do, then you invite the dangerous attitude that "the world owes you a living," as Phillips puts it. This tends to breed inertia, irresponsibility, and resentment.

Jason responded that he was ready to dive back into his efforts and asked if I could recommend any further reading. I told him: "First and foremost, I would get a good, original edition of *Think and Grow Rich* and read it through with great care—do everything with exactitude"—sound familiar?—"it is the best we've got. I would also read Emerson's essays *Self-Reliance*, *Spiritual Laws*, and *Compensation*. If you want to get a little experimental read Neville Goddard's *The Power of Awareness*." I also urged Jason to get a copy of *The Seven Laws of Money* and pay special attention to the first chapter, which deals with the question of financial survival.

But, above all, I counseled him: *begin*. Small but intelligent steps add a sense of personal agency to your efforts. We all need money, and we all must work out those needs—that is a given no matter what your situation in life. But do not allow money to deter the commencement of your plans. Do not.

TAKEAWAY POINTS:

- The act of writing down your aim has unexpected potency. Honor it.

- Your written aim is a sacred contract. Revise it until it is exactly right.

- Be sure that your DCA is clear and achievable, and that you have a complete grasp of all the factors involved.

- Read your statement of purpose with attentiveness, focus, and feeling at least once each day.

- Great execution matters more than great ideas.

- Imagination does not mean daydreaming. Imagination, plus organized plans, connects your knowledge and your ideas—it makes your knowledge useful.

- Reliable, specialized knowledge is crucial to your ability to carry out your project.

- You must turn specialized knowledge into actionable and organized plans.

- Seeking reliable information means carefully evaluating your sources. Never engage in cheap talk or listen to casual opinions.

- Experts can be wrong. Do your own research.

- Compromise is healthy as long as it does not violate the central purpose of your project.

- Follow Napoleon Hill's six steps to money. Do it with vigor and exactitude.

- Do not be a slave to money—but never be embarrassed to seek it. Money helps you attain your goals and safeguard your vision.

- Do not bind your DCA to your immediate financial survival. Achievement and survival are distinct concerns; tying one to the other will paralyze you.

5

Never Give Up: The Art of Intelligent Persistence

There are times when your Definite Chief Aim is going to seem out of reach. You will ask yourself: Is this working? Can I do this? Wouldn't I be better off setting my sights on something easier or more down-to-earth?

Persistence is an incredibly important part of achieving your DCA. Without it, you will fail. With it, you will be surprised by your successes at unexpected moments. Napoleon Hill taught that success often arrives just beyond the point where a "reasonable" person would give up.

It is also important to remember that *fulfillment often reaches you in unforeseen ways*. Your aim can seem extremely distant when you expect it to unfold, and for opportunities to reach you, in exactly one kind of way. Many salesmen have noted that their orders do not come from sales calls; they come peripherally—but when they stop making the calls the orders stop too. It is necessary to go through certain paces in order to generate business and connections, even though success arrives indirectly or unexpectedly. An underappreciated rule of success is: it often sneaks in, unannounced, through a back channel.

Napoleon Hill tells the story of legendary salesman Edwin C. Barnes, who is memorialized in *Think and Grow Rich*. Barnes's ambition was to work with Thomas Edison. He secured a menial job in Edison's New Jersey lab. When Edison invented his first Dictaphone machine, his sales force was indifferent. Nobody thought it would sell. Barnes moved in and got exclusive terms to sell the product, which became a success. It cemented his sales relationship with Edison. Success came because Barnes: 1) knew just what wanted (a partnership with Edison); and 2) placed himself in proximity to a project that no one else believed in.

The Law of Cycles

There is a special power to going about your business carefully, meticulously, and unceasingly—persevering at the work that is uniquely your own. Life is composed of cycles and when a cycle of opportunity reaches you, and you are prepared, the results are stellar.

Ralph Waldo Emerson and the Transcendentalists understood that our existence, the commerce of the world, and all human events mirror the cycles of nature. Life is seasonal, generatively repetitive, and cyclical. The demand for a certain service, product, or idea will manifest at a definite but unknown moment. Be prepared.

Mark Twain put it this way: "By the Law of Periodical Repetition, everything which has happened once must happen again and again and again—and not capriciously, but at regular periods, and each thing in its own period, not another's, and each obeying its own law . . . the same Nature which delights in periodical repetition in the skies is the Nature which orders the affairs of the earth. Let us not underrate the value of that hint."

Ecclesiastes 3:1 put it simply: "To everything there is a season."

It is not necessarily given to us to know the arc and patterns of these cycles. The bounce or opportunity you need will almost certainly arrive unexpectedly and after a great deal of sweat equity. Preparation alone allows you to make use of the opportunity when it comes. Emerson wrote that personal power consists of "concentration" and "drilling." He meant focusing your energies on a single goal (concentration), and persistently training, practicing, and perfecting your craft (drilling). This is what germ- theory pioneer Louis Pasteur was getting at when he said, "Chance favors the prepared mind."

Here are examples of some high achievers whose success reached them at unexpected moments, seemingly "out of the blue"—unless one thinks in terms of cycles. Each of these people was prepared and ready when destiny beckoned.

SOCIAL CRUSADER

The liberal evangelical activist Jim Wallace, editor of *Sojourners* magazine, spent the 1980s and 1990s writing books and articles on restoring the "social gospel" tradition to Christian culture. Jim was trying to get out the message that religious activists, in his view, needed to make more room for defending the poor and weak, and that non-religious activists needed to understand and embrace the social-justice teachings of Christianity. Jim's chief aim was to provide and promote a liberal alternative to the more conservative policies often associated with evangelical movements.

When George W. Bush became president in 2000, Democrats and liberals, many of whom hadn't heard Jim's name, grew concerned that they needed a better understanding of Christianity and politics, an area in which Bush was considered strong. Suddenly a whole new wave of readers, who hadn't been listening to Jim earlier, embraced his books and message. Jim's books shot to the top of the *New York Times* bestseller list and remained there for weeks. Jim himself hadn't changed. The times had. And suddenly a large audience discovered him, ready to listen to his case that political people of all stripes needed to better grasp and apply the social justice teachings of Christianity.

I watched it myself when this cycle hit. The events taught me that whatever you do in life, stand in your place and *do your work*. Don't change your tone or message for anyone else's benefit, or try to be "with the times." Plant your flag and go about your business. If your message is sound, the wheel of life, and of public opinion, will eventually reach you.

THE PHONE CALL
In 1967 the classically trained Canadian-American stage

actor Jonathan Frid (1924-2012) was preparing to quit the stage. Although Frid had landed some Broadway roles, he had grown tired of the boom-and-bust cycle that characterizes the work life of an actor. He wanted a steadier and more predictable livelihood. Frid was planning to leave New York City to open shop as a drama coach in Los Angeles, where acting teachers were in demand.

One day Frid was packing up his apartment when the phone rang. It was his agent asking him to read for the part of vampire on a low-budget, ratings-challenged gothic soap opera. The whole thing sounded silly to Frid. Preoccupied with his move, the actor refused. His agent persisted. Frid agreed to the audition. He got the part—and soon became famous as the guilt-plagued vampire Barnabas Collins on TV's *Dark Shadows*.

This is a phenomenon that Napoleon Hill called "three feet from gold." In *Think and Grow Rich*, Hill told the story of a mining engineer who quit his seemingly futile search for gold and sold his mine at a bargain price. The new owner struck a vein of gold—three feet from where his predecessor had stopped digging. This story exemplified Hill's principle that persistence delivers you. It is what happened to Jonathan Frid.

When Frid read for the part of Barnabas the producers immediately detected in the stage actor the kind of classical mien, and mixture of malevolence and vulnerability, that they sought for the role. Even after Frid accepted the job he expected it to be temporary, and arranged to delay, not cancel, his move. Barnabas was originally part of a subplot in the show's storyline. But viewers went wild over Frid as the agonized vampire. Ratings shot up and he became the show's main character.

Frid not only attained celebrity, but his portrayal of Barnabas as a tormented, near-sympathetic monster set the tone for the post-Dracula rendering of vampires by writers such as Anne Rice, who humanized the undead.

People sometimes refer to stories like Frid's as someone getting his "big break." But that doesn't really capture what happened. Years of training prepared the actor for the moment when his personal style and inflection were perfect for a once-in-a-lifetime role. Twenty years of effort preceded the phone call that day.

PERSEVERANCE CONQUERS

Minister and educator Russell H. Conwell (1843-1925) was determined to help working-class members of his Philadelphia parish attend college. In 1882 the minister began to teach students in the evenings in the basement of Grace Baptist Church. He also sent personal checks to college students to help them afford their studies.

But Conwell wanted to do more than tutor people in a basement and write checks. The minister was already known for his motivational lecture *Acres of Diamonds*, which defined success as filling a legitimate human need. In addition to his ministerial and teaching duties, Conwell maintaining an exhausting speaking schedule, delivering his *Acres of Diamonds* talk across the nation. One evening in an unfamiliar city he got an idea: He would dedicate his speaking fees, minus travel expenses, to establishing a college for working-class students.

In 1888 Conwell received a charter for the school that became Temple University in Philadelphia. To ensure the financial viability of his enterprise, Conwell continued giving his *Acres of Diamonds* talk and donating his fees to Temple. By his death in 1925 he had recited the speech more than 6,152 times.

Today Temple honors its founder with the official motto: *Perseverantia Vincit,* or Perseverance Conquers. It took Conwell just a single moment of insight—in this case dedicating his resources to a school for working-class students—to alter the face of higher learning in America, and secure his legacy as one of the nation's most innovative educators.

UNCOMMON COMMONSENSE

The legendary motivational writer Elbert Hubbard (1856-1915) began his career as a sales executive for a soap manufacturer. He dreamed of being a crusading social writer and novelist. In the early 1890s, Hubbard used a small fortune he had amassed from his share in the soap company to start a political and cultural magazine called *The Philistine,* as well as the artisan community Roycroft in East Aurora, New York.

In his writing, set against the upheaval of the industrial revolution and the urbanization of the country, Hubbard championed a call to commonsense values of fair play, equal justice, saying less and doing more, and restoring personal craftsmanship to products, which he practiced at the Roycroft workshops. Hubbard inveighed against child labor and sweatshops. He criticized the "sophisticated" modern mindset, which resulted in collegians who were educated in everything except useful, skilled crafts and jobs, which Hubbard believed were undervalued in the new industrial economy

By the turn of the century, however, Hubbard had found only middling success as a writer. But one evening at a family dinner in February 1899, Hubbard had an idea that made him, for a time, one of the most famous writers in the world.

The publisher and his son discussed the experience of Lieutenant Andrew S. Rowan, an intelligence officer in US Army during the Spanish-American War. At the outset of the conflict in 1898, Rowan was ordered to deliver a vital US military message to General Calixto Garcia, the leader of a rebellion against Spanish rule of Cuba. All that was known of Garcia's whereabouts was that he was hunkered down at a jungle base somewhere in eastern Cuba. With little strategic briefing or material help from the US Army, Rowan landed on the island, located the rebel general, and delivered his "message to Garcia," which was a vital piece of military intelligence that solidified the US alliance with Cuban partisans, and led to Spain's defeat.

Hubbard was deeply taken with the character of Lieutenant Rowan. The officer displayed independence of thought, resourcefulness, and determination. Those traits, Hubbard reasoned, were in alarmingly short supply in the lives of most working people, who quickly vacillated from excitement to boredom, and often did their jobs with apathy.

Hubbard needed to fill a bit of blank space in *The Philistine*. So, after dinner, in the space of one hour, he produced what he called a "literary trifle" on the virtues of Rowan, and used the essay to plug up his empty column in the March 1899 issue. The piece was so minor to him that he ran it without a headline. But the brief statement quickly gained national attention. Employers, managers, college presidents, and generals ordered reprints of the issue or paid to reprint the Garcia piece as a pamphlet—first by the thousands and eventually (and quite literally) the millions. The essay, which Hubbard later titled *A Message to Garcia*, became so popular that for many years the term "carry a message to Garcia" was slang for attempting a challenging task. The essay got translated around the world and was read by foreign armies and workforces. Parents gave copies to children who were starting college or entering the job market. Enterprising clerks, with eyes on the corner office, gobbled up copies.

A Message to Garcia remained a mainstay of American success literature for close to fifty years. While the work's popularity today is nowhere near what it once was, it remains possible to find the occasional employer who still gives copies to new hires. A friend recently told me that his daughter received a copy from an old accountant the day she started working for him.

A Message to Garcia made Hubbard a household name in America, and brought attention to everything that he said and wrote thereafter. Hubbard's essay was not only one of the first mass-read works of motivational literature, but it set the template for the entire field of business motivation as it exists today.

Hubbard and his wife Alice died in 1915 when a German U-boat sunk a passenger liner that they taking to Europe to protest World War One to the German Kaiser. The tragic ending to Hubbard's life in no way reduces, and in many ways reflects, the dynamism and relevance that marked his existence. Hubbard's ability to make his voice heard internationally grew from an hour's work one night—an hour, one could add, for which he had been preparing all his life.

When reflecting on all of these figures and their achievements, consider this precept from Jewish sage Menachem Mendel Schneerson (1902-1994), known as the Rebbe: "All good things come unexpectedly." To which I would add: but only to him who is prepared.

Eight Habits of Highly Persistent People

"Persistence is a state of mind," Napoleon Hill wrote, "therefore it can be cultivated." Hill taught that persistence is based on eight character traits found in resilient people.

Read over these traits with complete honesty. Which of these qualities do you possess? Where you are deficient? It will be profitable to dedicate eight days to studying these traits in yourself, focusing on one each day. Get a small notebook and make notes throughout the day as to when you exemplified or fell short of a given trait. Pay careful attention to deficiencies that need strengthening.

1. **Definiteness of Purpose**. This may seem like a no-brainer since the whole book is based on this topic. But use this as an opportunity to test yourself. Nothing builds persistence better than being certain about *exactly what you want*. That alone surmounts many difficulties.

2.   **Desire**. If your desire is sufficiently strong and impassioned you will naturally pursue your objective with persistence. If your persistence wanes, check whether you want your objective badly enough.

3.   **Self-Reliance**. This phrase is widely heard and rarely understood. Read Ralph Waldo Emerson's famous essay of the same name. Self-reliance is not selfishness or stubbornness. It is independent purpose, nonconformity, and realistic self-belief.

4.   **Definiteness of Plans**. You are better able to apply yourself if your plans are definite, simple, and clear. Specificity aids persistence.

5.   **Accurate Knowledge**. "*Guessing* instead of *knowing* destroys persistence," Hill wrote. Your plans must rest on sound knowledge and accurate information (these things come from experience, observation, and research). Accuracy builds confidence.

6.   **Cooperation**. Only a fool tries to go it alone. You must get along with coworkers, employees, partners, clients, vendors, and buyers. No one acts in a vacuum.

7.   **Will Power**. Like Self-reliance, will power is often misunderstood. It means *concentrating* your thoughts, plans, and energies on a definite, single purpose.

8. **Habit**. Some habits are innate; others arise from the *repetition of acts*. You can cultivate persistence as a desirable habit. Repetition of purposeful and industrious acts builds persistence. The more you persist, the more natural it becomes.

I now want to note the opposite character traits that Hill said kill persistence:

1. Failure to recognize and clearly define what you want.
2. Procrastination of any kind.
3. Lack of interest in acquiring specialized knowledge.
4. Indecision.
5. Failure to make clear, definite plans.
6. Self-satisfaction.
7. Willingness to compromise or "give in" at all times.
8. Blaming others for your mistakes
9. Weakness of desire.
10. Willingness to quit at the first sign of defeat.
11. Lack of written plans.
12. Neglecting to seize opportunity when it appears.
13. Idle wishing, talking, or daydreaming.
14. Compromising with poverty instead of aiming at riches. General absence of ambition to *be*, to *do*, and to *own*.
15. Searching for short cuts to success; trying to *get* without *giving*.
16. Fear of criticism.

An Experiment in Growth

When Napoleon Hill told the story of Andrew Carnegie challenging him as a young journalist to make a comprehensive study of the nature of success, the idea was only an abstraction. "It was," Hill wrote, "a favorable 'break' that gave me the biggest opportunity of my life—*but*— twenty-five years of *determined effort* had to be devoted to that opportunity before it became an asset."

Do you have the endurance to invest that kind of effort? So much depends on how passionately you want your goal. "It was," Hill wrote, "no ordinary DESIRE that survived disappointment, discouragement, temporary defeat, criticism, and the constant reminding of 'waste of time.' It was a BURNING DESIRE! An OBSESSION!" I repeat this point because it is of inestimable importance to your success.

You may find that, powerful as your desire is, there are periods where you feel defeated. Whenever you are ready to give up, here is a special step—a motivational 911 call—that can rescue you from discouragement and despair. In the fall of 2015 I began an ongoing experiment, which I now invite you to join. I call it the Thirty-Day Mental Challenge. In articles, talks, and media appearances I dared people to write out and sign a personal pledge to focus for thirty days, to the absolute best of their ability, on whatever is advancing, affirming, and constructive in their lives, both past and present. During this period, you are to consider every reasonable ambition within reach. You are to drop all grudges, inner arguments, and complaining. Thirty days. No bull. No wavering. See what happens.

I gave participants an email address, which I will also give you, to report their results to me. I personally replied to everyone who wrote in. I received a great number of emails—some people reported breakthroughs, some reported difficulties, and some asked probing questions. But not one person who responded was unmoved by the exercise. I urge you to approach this exercise with deep seriousness. It may make a remarkable difference in your life. It can be repeated any time—whenever you feel stuck, alone, or in need of a renewal of your energy and enthusiasm in pursuit of your aim.

Since I have the advantage of greater space in this book than in the column where I first introduced the mental challenge, I am expanding and providing fuller detail for maximum benefit. Here is the background, inspiration, and one vital step for you to take.

Thirty-Day Mental Challenge

American philosopher William James (1842-1910) yearned to find a practical spirituality, one that produced concrete improvements in happiness. The Harvard physician grew encouraged, especially in his final years, by his personal experiments with positive-mind metaphysics, or New Thought. James called it "the religion of healthy-mindedness." In this experiment, we will continue James's search for a testable, workable philosophy of living.

The experiment is based on a passage from a 1931 book, *Body, Mind, and Spirit* by Elwood Worcester and Samuel McComb. The authors, both Episcopal ministers, were founders of the Emmanuel Movement, a respected healing ministry in the early decades of the twentieth century. The Emmanuel Movement was named for Emmanuel Church in Boston's Back Bay, where its members met. Worcester and McComb, joint pastors of the church, brought together ministers, physicians, psychologists, and patients to study and apply the recuperative abilities of the mind.

In *Body, Mind, and Spirit*, a prominent scientist, who the authors did not name, told a small audience of how he radically improved his life through a one-month thought experiment. Here, with a few excisions, is his testimony:

> Ladies and gentlemen, before I sit down I wish to make a more personal statement which I think you will find of greater value and interest than my lecture. Up to my fiftieth year (he is now about sixty-five) I was an unhappy, ineffective man. None of the works on which my reputation rests was published. I was making my home in an unimportant town in California and was utterly unknown in the scientific world. I lived in a constant sense of gloom and failure. Perhaps my most painful symptom was a blinding headache, which recurred usually two days of the week, during which I could do nothing.
>
> As my fiftieth birthday approached, I began to take stock of my soul and I realized that something was very wrong with me. I had read some of the literature of New Thought, which at the time appeared to be buncombe, and some statements of William James on the directing

of attention to what is good and useful and ig-
noring the rest. One saying of his stuck in my
mind, 'We might have to give up our philosophy of evil, but what is that in comparison with
gaining a life of goodness?' (or words to that
effect). Hitherto these doctrines had seemed to
me only mystical theories, but realizing that my
soul was sick and growing worse and that my
life was intolerable, I determined to put them
to the proof. In accordance with my teaching
and mental habits, I resolved to make a careful,
honest experiment which should be as carefully and honestly recorded. I decided to limit
the period of conscious effort to one month, as I
thought this time long enough to prove its value
or its worthlessness to me. During this month
I resolved to impose certain restrictions on my
thoughts. If I thought of the past, I would try
to let my mind dwell only on its happy, pleasing
incidents, the bright days of my childhood, the
inspiration of my teachers and the slow revelation of my life-work. In thinking of the present,
I would deliberately turn my attention to its desirable elements, my home, the opportunities
my solitude gave me to work, and so on, and I
resolved to make the utmost use of these opportunities and to ignore the fact that they seemed
to lead to nothing. In thinking of the future I
determined to regard every worthy and possible
ambition as within my grasp. Ridiculous as this
seemed at the time, in view of what has come to
me since, I see that the only defect of my plan

was that it aimed too low and did not include enough.

By this time I felt that I was about to make an important discovery and I began to be conscious of a certain tingling of expectation which I usually experience in my scientific work at such moments. When the day I had assigned arrived, I threw myself into the new task (incomparably the greatest I had ever attempted to perform) with ardor. I did not have to wait a month. At the end of eight days, I knew that the experiment was succeeding. I had not thought of including my headaches in my scheme of effort, as I deemed these beyond the possibility of help from this source. But therein I miscalculated, as they abruptly ceased. In fifteen years I have had but one headache and that was one I deliberately brought on for experimental purposes.

Apart from this welcome relief, the first change of which I was aware was that whereas for many years I had been profoundly unhappy, I now felt happy and contented. I knew what James meant when he spoke of 'being consciously right and superior.' What surprised me more was that I was able to make others happy and that my personality seemed to attract, whereas before it had repelled. Up to this point of my recital I anticipate that you will find nothing strange in these changes and discoveries, expect that I made them so late in life. What follows may tax your credulity. Personally I should not have accepted one of these statements sixteen years ago.

Yet most of the changes in my outer life are matters of fact, which can be verified in *Who's Who*. As I stated at the beginning, the burdens I found hardest to bear were my obscurity and isolation, consciousness that the passing years were bringing me no nearer the goal of my ambition, that although my capacity was considerable, my name was unknown and my works unpublished because no publisher would accept them.

The outward changes of my life resulting from my change of thought have surprised me more than the inward changes, yet they sprang from the latter. There were certain eminent men, for example, whose recognition I deeply craved. The foremost of these wrote me, out of a clear sky, and invited me to become his assistant. My works have all been published, and a foundation has been created to publish all that I may write in the future. The men with whom I have worked have been helpful and cooperative toward me chiefly on account of my changed disposition. Formerly they would not have endured me. One ambition of mine, my election to the presidency of a great foreign scientific society, though in accordance with my highest hope, seemed so utterly beyond my reach that I should have dreamed it preposterous to aim at it, yet it came to me. As I look back over all these changes, it seems to me that in some blind way I stumbled on a *path of life* and set forces to working for me which before were working against me.

*   *   *

Let's repeat this experiment together. Chose your start date, and write out the following passage: "I dedicate myself on this day of _____ to focus on all that is nourishing, advancing, and promising for thirty days. I will read this vow three times daily: on awakening, at midday, and before going to sleep. I commit myself with all my energies and devotion to this task for thirty days, for the good of all concerned. (signed) _____"

I recommend writing this passage on an index card, and on the reverse creating a grid in which you mark off each of your thirty days. It may also help to reread the scientist's testimony each time you mark off a day, or whenever you feel it necessary. When you catch yourself sliding into old habits of thought, do not worry; simply steer yourself back to the experiment. You do not need to start over. Just carry on.

Email me your results (or questions) at 30DayMental Challenge@gmail.com.

Bumps in Your Experiment

Let me note that this experiment has certain inherent difficulties. One of them—and I want you to watch for this in yourself—is that we actually enjoy outrage, anger, grudges, and the reenacting of past arguments or suffering. Why? Who would *want* to feel badly? Well, there's more to it than that: We experience a distinctive thrill and excitement when we indulge in emotions of anger and fear. We get entranced by looking at what angers or frightens us, like watching a horror movie. The experience gives us a jolt of novelty and excitement, as well as a wash of relief that the monster isn't presently real and in front of us.

More so, we derive a sense of satisfaction—and, in many cases, even our sense of selfhood and identity—from rerunning disasters, past or imagined, in our minds. We like to plot out what we would say or do if a certain situation presented itself. Although we would deny it, we often wish for conflict to reappear so that we can play the avenging hero or take revenge.

Sometimes we rerun conflicts in hopes of a finding an answer to what went wrong—but this is generally a depleting exercise, and simply places us back in the orbit of the original problem. We see this in the extraordinary movie *The Deer Hunter*, when a tormented Vietnam veteran and former POW played by Christopher Walken willingly returns to a game of Russian roulette, which his Vietcong captors had once forced on him. He is hopelessly and dangerously trying to make sense of what happened to him. And perhaps even trying to regain the feeling of aliveness that the horrible experience gave him.

Have you ever overheard someone on a cellphone describing to a friend how angry he is at someone at work or at home? Have you noticed how indignant the speaker sounds? He is lost in his own drama in which he is innocent and unjustly wounded, telling the world how unfairly he was treated. Now, think how *you* sound when you are in your own head, rerunning an argument or confrontation, imagining what you would say and how you would say it. Although it is a fantasy, you have a feeling of triumph, bigness, and pride in striking back. Your body is flooded with adrenaline. You are lost in your drama, unaware of other things or people around you. However momentarily thrilling the experience can feel, the longterm effects, on your physiology, psyche, and life circumstances, are devastating. These habits of thought cement our gravitational center in a place of anger rather than one of ideas and productivity. And our thoughts, as with all that we focus on, get reenacted through autosuggestion, often without our awareness.

Watch yourself carefully as you embark on this challenge. Mental habits are trenchant, and often pull us toward the negative. It is not your fault; it is how we are conditioned. Negative emotions can be a form of addiction. The body, for example, can grow to crave the release of adrenaline. In many cases, our negativity gets habituated to the point where we lack a sense of self unless we are reacting in fear and anger, plotting an escape or counter-argument. Negative emotions can rule our lives.

This is why you must approach the thirty-day challenge with commitment and seriousness. Notice that the scientist said he threw himself into it with ardor and zeal. Do the same. One of the things that can help generate this sense of zeal, and help you maintain your resolve during the thirty days, is having a specific goal that you are aiming to gain through the exercise. What do you want most right now? What do you want with burning passion? Put some skin in the game. The point of the experiment is to see what changes manifest in your life, or what benefits come to you. Be completely practical about it. This is a philosophy of results.

A student once asked Napoleon Hill how he could possibly control his thoughts and emotions during a state of intense anger. The question is very pertinent. Hill replied, *"In exactly the same way that you would change your manner and tone if you were in a heated argument with a family member and heard the doorbell ring, signaling that company was about to visit. You would control yourself because you would desire to.*" As a rule we generally cannot control our emotions. But control, of a sort, does appear when one emotion gets pitted against another, stronger emotion. If you have ever found it necessary to quickly conceal your feelings and change your facial expression for some larger aim—such avoiding embarrassment at work or in public—you know that it can be done. This is why you must approach the challenge with some kind of deeply held desire in mind. Pit your desire against the negative emotions that will naturally come up—and continue.

As I am writing these words I am resuming the thirty-day challenge myself. I have a passionately felt, specific desire that is in harmony with my definite aim. Holding this desire helps me focus on my purpose and drives my commitment during the thirty days. Focus on what you achingly want to receive. Make it concrete. That is the decisive factor.

Five Powerful Words

Here is a small but meaningful tip to use during the Thirty-Day Mental Challenge, and afterwards. It comes from a short line in the novel *Atlas Shrugged* by capitalist philosopher Ayn Rand.

Rand was a fierce individualist who believed that understanding and attaining your purpose in life is the highest expression of existence. The person who lacks a purpose is, in Rand's view, immoral. Whatever one thinks of the broader implications of Rand's ideas, it is well worth becoming familiar with her work if only to appreciate the deep value she placed on seeing through your vision as an artist, businessperson, or whatever vocation to which you are dedicated.

In Rand's novel, one of her heroes, steel magnate and inventor Hank Reardon, is facing opposition and injustice from all sides as he is attempting to market a new, vastly superior form of steel. When problems threaten to cloud Hank's mind and disrupt his purpose, he thinks: "It must not stop me."

Read those five words again. Make them your mantra while you are pursuing the Thirty-Day Mental Challenge, and at other times. You are not necessarily required to think rosy thoughts when hit with, or reminded of, problems. But you are required to exercise *determined thought*. When your mind drifts, as it invariably will, back to insults (real or perceived), past problems, unfairness, or current difficulties do this: Consider your Definite Chief Aim and inwardly *feel* these five words: **It Must Not Stop Me.**

If you are passionate for your aim this small step can prove very powerful.

Persistence and Faith

Napoleon Hill wrote of the need to proceed with "faith." But this can be difficult for some people to understand. Although I am a religious person, I have difficulty with the concept of faith. The close friend and collaborator of a famous minister, well known to millions of people, once told me that when this man was on his deathbed one of his children exclaimed in perplexity, "Daddy has no faith!"

I don't judge that minister, or anyone else who has had this experience. When I heard the story I conceded to the man telling me: "I am same way—I have been a seeker for many years, and a believer, but I don't think I have what you would call 'faith'." To me, faith seems passive. So, let me suggest a different way of looking at it, which you may find helpful if you are a nonbeliever or, like me, a believer who has problems with the concept of faith.

Any time you encounter the term "faith"—either in this book or in any of Napoleon Hill's writing—substitute in its place the word "persistence." You will be surprised how well it fits. "FAITH and FEAR," Hill wrote—one constructive, the other destructive—"make poor bedfellows. *Where one is found, the other cannot exist.*" If you substitute persistence for faith, Hill's statement takes on a new dimension of meaning. Persistence is a quality of extraordinary power; it is neither mysterious nor requiring of a transcendent experience. It is a work ethic.

Novelist Herman Wouk credited William Faulkner with saying: "I only write when inspiration strikes. Fortunately it strikes at nine every morning." I like that ethic. It rejects airy-fairy rituals about doing one's work, whether as an artist, professional, or businessperson. There is just the act of doing it. Acting in this way— in which persistence becomes your faith—will come to you more naturally and easily when you love what you're doing. Hence, the omnipresent importance of a DCA that fills you with passion.

The Master Mind

One of the most important steps of Napoleon Hill's program—and one that will greatly help your march toward your DCA—is the formation of a Master Mind group. An entire volume in this series is devoted to the Master Mind. That's how important it was to Hill's philosophy.

Napoleon Hill defined the Master Mind as: "Coordination of knowledge and effort, in a spirit of harmony, between two or more people for the attainment of a definite purpose." It really means meeting regularly, and in coordinated effort, with others to explore and support one another's plans, purposes, and needs. Hill believed that an amalgamation of minds amounted to more than the sum of each. If several people regularly meet in a spirit of comity, harmony, and mutual support (there can be no divisiveness in the Master Mind) it will serve to amp up the creativity, intuition, and mental faculties of each member of the group.

Ralph Waldo Emerson termed this process the "Over-Soul," the title of one of his essays. Hill believed deeply in the efficacy of a Master Mind group, and insisted that no lasting success was possible without this vital resource. In an age of pinched schedules and digital isolation, it is tempting to neglect this step. Do not.

As noted, your Master Mind group may consist of any number from two or higher (but no more than seven, which gets unwieldy). Select the members of your Master Mind group carefully—the key factor is harmony and cooperation. You may focus on a single group goal, or, more likely, each member may have his own personal aims. Arrange a time to meet regularly to discuss your plans and ideas, and to exchange advice and guidance. When you're not together, hold each member's wishes and needs in your mind.

In this cyber-age people often live and work at far distances. My own Master Mind group is dispersed from New England to Southern California. We structure things this way: Its five participants, all possessed of supportive natures, good humor, and spiritual values, meet at a regularly designated time by conference call once each week. We begin by reading a short statement of principles, and then each member individually offers a piece of personal good news from the previous week. Each member then takes a turn describing his wants and needs for the week ahead. After a member has expressed his wants and needs, each group member offers advice, ideas, encouragement, and often prayer or other forms of support. The call is generally under one hour.

This friendly alliance, if carried out with purpose and harmony, will, in time, yield extraordinary results. For example, everyone in a Master Mind group, Hill taught, gains heightened insight through the subconscious minds of all the other members. This produces a more vivid imaginative and mental state in which new ideas "flash" into your awareness, he taught. There are also practical benefits in which economic and business issues are hashed out and discussed.

I can honestly say that our Master Mind group—and I know all of its members would agree—has been one of the most helpful and dynamic aspects in each of our lives. Our meetings steady me when I am off course, and give me fresh perspective and an added boost to the week. And there is something more. "No two minds,"

Hill wrote, "ever come together without, thereby, creating a third invisible, intangible force which may be likened to a third mind." This, to him, was the "psychic" phase of the Master Mind, in which the mind may be likened to an energy that is pooled with that of others to intensify intuitions, ideas, and insights. Whether you are ready to make the leap to this way of thought, I can promise you that from every perspective the Master Mind will play an invaluable and practical role in your pursuit of success.

"Great power," Hill insisted, "can be accumulated through no other principle."

ACTION STEP:
Your Confidence Pledge

Intelligent persistence requires realistic self-belief. Here is a personal pledge adapted from Napoleon Hill's first book, *The Law of Success*, that helps to build and sustain healthful confidence. Consider this pledge carefully—and then write it down and sign your name to it.

Repeat this pledge at least once a day until it becomes part of your mental makeup. Keep a copy of it as a daily reminder. By doing so you will again be making use of autosuggestion—or self-suggestion—to develop the crucial trait of confidence.

Never mind what anyone may say about your method. Outside of your Master Mind group (with whom you should be able to share everything) you do not have to talk to anyone about it. It's best not to. Just remember that it is your aim to succeed, and that this creed, if mastered and applied, will aid you.

I believe in myself. I believe in my coworkers. I believe in my employer. I believe in my friends. I believe in my family. I believe that God will lend me everything I need to succeed if I do my best to earn it through faithful and honest service. I believe in prayer and will never close my eyes in sleep without praying for divine guidance to be patient with others and tolerant of those who do not believe as I do. I believe that success is the result of intellectual effort and does not depend upon blind luck or sharp-practices or double-crossing. I believe that I will get from life what I put into it, therefore I will conduct myself toward others as I would want them to act toward me. I will not spread or listen to slander and gossip. I will not slight my work no matter what I may see others doing. I will render the best service possible because I have pledged myself to succeed in life, and I know that true success is the result of conscientious and efficient effort. Finally, I will forgive those who offend me because I realize that I shall sometimes offend others and I will need their forgiveness.

Remember: Write this statement out, sign it, recite it daily, and keep it where you can see it.

TAKEAWAY POINTS:

- Fulfillment and success often arrive through unexpected channels. Allow for varying possibilities.

- Life is cyclical. Success often comes after you do exceptional work and stand right where you are. People and circumstances eventually cycle toward you.

- Remember the Rebbe's saying: "All good things come unexpectedly."

- Study the eight habits that Napoleon Hill associated with intelligent persistence, and the sixteen traits that kill persistence.

- Do the Thirty-Day Mental Challenge—and do it with everything in you.

- "It must not stop me"—that is the motto of persistence.

- The Master Mind is an essential step. Do not fool yourself into thinking that it's secondary or can wait till "later." It is vital to your efforts.

6

When Wishes Fail

At the beginning of this book I promised you that I do not sell fantasies. I meant it. Hence, I cannot conclude this study without considering the question of failure. Even when you feel that you've been intelligently persistent and have done everything right, there are times when you will reasonably conclude that you have failed.

I cannot pretend that this doesn't happen, or that every event in life feels like some kind of a stepping-stone, or at least not when it first transpires. But failure is not cause for inertia. It must not be. The only true failure, as Napoleon Hill taught, comes when you give up. That might sound platitudinous or corny, but I believe in my heart that it is true. I would add to it that failure also comes only when you have lost all sense of work ethic, purpose, and ideals. If you haven't lost those three things, you can reliably find a new road.

To illustrate this, I want to invoke the career of one of the most unusual figures of recent American history: Edgar Cayce (1887-1945). Sometimes called the grandfather of alternative medicine, Cayce was a devout Christian born and raised in Kentucky. While warm and humble in person, he had a controversial and inscrutable gift: from within a trance state Cayce appeared able to diagnose and prescribe cures for illnesses, often at long distances and for subjects he did not know. In his more than 14,000 trance readings, Cayce laid out some of the key elements of what later became known as holistic medicine and transpersonal psychology.

Although Cayce has a wide range of admirers today, and his works are read around the world, there was a time in his career when circumstances seemed to have dealt him a crippling blow. It is within this episode that we will find universal lessons on how to reemerge from failure.

The Path Out of Failure

In winter of 1931 the medical clairvoyant Cayce came to feel that his life's work had amounted to nothing. A dedicated Christian, Cayce had long dreamed of establishing a hospital based on his health readings. But in February the healer's Virginia Beach hospital and research center ran out of operating money and was forced to close its doors, less than two years after opening. Patients had to leave, files were carted off, and Cayce wandered the halls alone gathering his personal belongings before the building was shuttered.

The financial collapse arrived after longtime contributors quarreled with Cayce and abruptly abandoned him and his work. The Great Depression did the rest to gut his 30-bed facility.

"I've been tested," Cayce told his wife Gertrude. "And I've failed."

Today, the original hospital building is not only back in the hands of the organization that Cayce founded, the Association for Research and Enlightenment (A.R.E.), but has recently undergone a remodeling and is now a bustling facility that houses a school of massage, a health spa, classrooms, the offices of Atlantic University, and a health-food restaurant that ranks with dining experiences in "crunchy capitals" like San Francisco and Boulder, CO.

The new health facility is sleekly designed and comfortable. I recently had the opportunity to speak there with actress Lindsay Wagner, TV's "Bionic Woman," as part of a program presented at the Cayce visitors' center, also beautifully designed with up-to-date television studio facilities.

Cayce's dream of a holistic health center is flourishing in ways that he wouldn't have imagined back in the grim winter of 1931. How did this turnaround occur?

Months after the hospital's closing, while Cayce remained withdrawn and depressed, his eldest son, Hugh Lynn, then 24, approached him with an idea to reconstitute the Cayce work. As Hugh Lynn saw it, his father needed to free himself from dependency on one or two big donors, as well as from fly-by-night seekers. Instead, Hugh Lynn envisioned a member-supported organization that would keep people involved in all facets of his father's work—personal healing, spiritual growth, and self-development—while also providing a steady base of member support.

In essence, Hugh Lynn called for self-determination. He wanted the newly formed ARE to demonstrate: 1) financial independence, with a scrappy willingness to do as much, or as little, as its member-based budget permitted; and 2) intellectual integrity, with a determination to organize, verify, and cross-reference the Cayce readings so that patients and seekers were not treated in isolation. Hugh Lynn's formula transformed temporary defeat into renewed action and lasting purpose. Hugh Lynn's program is every bit as serviceable and broadly applicable for anyone facing setback today as it was for his father in the early 1930s. Here is what Hugh Lynn told Edgar Cayce, as recounted by family friend and biographer Thomas Sugrue:

> "Maybe there's something wrong with us. Suppose we stop expecting people to do things for us and start doing them for ourselves. The world doesn't owe us a living . . . we ought to work for what we get just as everyone else does.
>
> "In the first place, we don't know anything about the thing we're trying to sell. We look at the information as if it were a faucet. Just turn the tap and whatever we want flows out. We were going to give the world our wisdom—the wisdom that came out of the faucet when we turned the tap. We figured it was our wisdom because we had the faucet.
>
> "We don't know anything about psychic

phenomena. We have our own experiences, but we don't know what else has been done in the field.

"What do we know about the Life Readings? Do we know the history well enough to check the periods mentioned for people and give them a bibliography—a list of books and articles—with each reading? Certainly not!

"Do we know enough about philosophy, metaphysics, and comparative religion to check the readings on what is said in these fields?

"When a reading makes a statement and says it is a philosophical truth, do we know what philosophers believed the same thing, and what religions have it in their dogma?

"When a statement about anatomy, or about a disease, or about the use of a medicine or herb is made, do we know whether medical authorities believe the same thing or condemn it, or know nothing of the matter?

"If a person asked us for everything the readings have said about appendicitis, or ulcers of the stomach, or migraine, or the common cold, or epilepsy, or marriage, or forgiveness of sin, or love, could we produce it? Certainly not. That work was barely begun when the hospital closed.

"I think it would be wise if we stopped looking for large donations, stopped dreaming of another hospital, and concentrated on developing a little stock-in-trade. Then, when the next change comes, we'll be better prepared and we won't muff it."

"I don't know how to do that sort of work—" Edgar began.

"You don't have to," Hugh Lynn said. "I'll do it . . . I'll take over the job of manager of the Association. We'll keep it small; we'll have a modest budget and a modest program.

"We'll work quietly, by ourselves, with the help of the local people who are interested. We'll start study groups. We'll take series of readings on various subjects. We'll build up a library on psychic phenomena.

"Then when people come and ask what we do, we can say something other than that we take two readings a day, send them to people who pay for them, and put copies in our files. That isn't much for an organization that goes around under the name of the Association for Research and Enlightenment."

Leaving aside the question of Cayce's work, I ask you to consider how Hugh Lynn's ideas can be applied in your own life. I find four principles in his statement:

1. **Self-Sufficiency.** As much as possible, cultivate a sense of realistic self-reliance. Are your plans or projects rightly scaled, or are they overly dependent upon the resources and approval of others? Outsiders can withdraw their support just as quickly as they give it. Build on solid foundations.

2. **Higher Vision.** Regularly check yourself to be certain that your plans are based on the ethical

certainty of serving something higher, and interjecting real benefit into the world.

3.   **Steady Goes It**. Build your projects patiently and methodically. Be willing to do as much, or as little, as resources permit. This is not only practical but also grants you the satisfaction of knowing that you are functioning without damaging compromises and within your own means.

4.   **Sweat Equity**. Constantly ask: Am I performing my work with the highest quality and integrity? Do I suffuse my work with the skill and effort necessary to provide the finest possible service?

ACTION STEP:
Essentials to Remember

When you are recovering from failure—which Hill always called "temporary defeat"—and are forming new plans or revising old ones, reflect on these eleven major attributes of leadership. Hill identified these traits as common to all great achievers:

1. Unwavering Courage
2. Self-Control
3. A Keen Sense of Justice
4. Definiteness of Decision
5. Definiteness of Plans
6. The Habit of Doing More Than Paid For

7. A Pleasing Personality
8. Sympathy and Understanding
9. Mastery of Detail
10. Willingness to Assume Full Responsibility
11. Cooperation With Others

Consider each of these traits carefully. Which of them would your spouse or significant other say are your weakest? What would your workmates say? What would your children or siblings say? It may be that your weakness in one or more of these areas is like a riptide carrying you away from your aim, regardless of how hard you swim toward it. Many of these traits are expanded upon in the appendix, The Sixteen Laws of Success.

Am I Aiming High Enough?

It may seem counterintuitive, but aiming *too low* can form a barrier to success. You might not be dealing with the right kinds of people or people with the right talents, you might not be reaching decision makers, you might not be exposing yourself to the relationships, leads, publicity, and word of mouth that would come from presenting your idea, service, or product on a larger stage.

This kind of thing happened to me. While I was working on my first book in 2007, I continued to write articles on alternative spiritual topics for various magazines. But I was unhappy with how my pieces were being published. Small magazines in the alternative spiritual culture were sometimes burying my pieces deep inside, and not featuring them on the cover. I felt that my work was of high quality and deserved better exposure. I was stuck and did not know what to do.

One day I was having lunch with my friend Mark Thurston, a writer and teacher who has made a lifelong study of the psycho-spiritual ideas of Edgar Cayce. I told Mark about my problem. He reply was exquisitely simple, and it turned on a light for me: "It sounds like you need to be writing for better magazines." It hadn't occurred to me. Perhaps the pieces were getting sold short because they were in the wrong places. I needed to step up my professional relationships, exposure, and venues. In the years immediately ahead I got published in *The Washington Post, The Wall Street Journal,* and *U.S. News and World Report,* among others. In years still further I wrote for *The New York Times,* Salon, Politico, Time.com, CNN.com, and elsewhere. I went from writing for small, subculture magazines—and feeling that my work wasn't being properly valued—to having bylines in some of the most widely read publications in America, and on the kinds of topics that are not often found in the national media.

What changed? Thanks to Mark's comment, I simply realized that I could, and needed to, expand my sense of where my work should appear. I was dedicated to writing serious articles on alternative spiritual topics. I believed then, as I still do, that coverage of counter-cultural spiritual topics should be produced and published with the same quality and discrimination brought to coverage of any mainstream topic. All I needed to do was take this commitment into the broader culture. I did—and it worked.

Here is Napoleon Hill on his personal experience:

Too many people refuse to set high goals for themselves, or even neglect selecting a career, because they fear the criticism of relatives and "friends" who may say "Don't aim so high, people will think you are crazy."

When Andrew Carnegie suggested that I devote twenty years to the organization of a philosophy of individual achievement my first impulse of thought was fear of what people might say. The suggestion set up a goal for me, far out of proportion to any I had ever conceived. As quick as a flash, my mind began to create alibis and excuses, all of them traceable to the inherent FEAR OF CRITICISM. Something inside of me said, "You can't do it—the job is too big, and requires too much time—what will your relatives think of you?—how will you earn a living?—no one has ever organized a philosophy of success, what right have you to believe you can do it?—who are you, anyway, to aim so high?—remember your humble birth—what do you know about philosophy—people will think you are crazy—(and they did)—why hasn't some other person done this before now?

These, and many other questions flashed into my mind, and demanded attention. It seemed as if the whole world had suddenly turned its attention to me with the purpose of ridiculing me into giving up all desire to carry out Mr. Carnegie's suggestion.

I had a fine opportunity, then and there, to kill off ambition before it gained control of me. Later in life, after having analyzed thousands of people, I discovered that MOST IDEAS ARE STILL-BORN, AND NEED THE BREATH OF LIFE INJECTED INTO THEM THROUGH DEFINITE PLANS OF IMMEDIATE ACTION. The time to nurse an idea is at the time of its birth. Every minute it lives, gives it a better chance of surviving.

I urge you to consider whether you have been bold enough in pursuit of your work—and whether you have brought your work onto a large enough stage, or given it the fullest exposure. Don't get me wrong: I believe in starting small. I did myself. I also believe in following what might be called the "blue-collar path to success"—taking it slow and steady and paying your dues. But you should regularly check in with yourself to consider whether you have outgrown the flowerpot in which you're planted. Consider whether you are receiving enough sun, soil, and nutrients to bring your work into the broader world. If not, aim higher.

Coping With Tragedy

There are no soothing words for the tragedies that life sometimes visits upon us. Accidents, illnesses, or unforeseen events can upend everything we thought we had planned for. John Lennon adapted a popular adage in his song *Beautiful Boy*: "Before you cross the street take my hand. Life is what happens to you while you're busy making other plans."

Those words are especially poignant coming from

an artist who, twelve hours before his 1980 assassination, told an interviewer: "It's not out of our control. I still believe in love, peace . . . I still believe in positive thinking." Lennon's statement should not be read sardonically. It is a statement of ideals from a man who acknowledged life's unknowns.

If you suddenly find yourself living with extraordinary difficulty, your aims or priorities may have to radically change. Recovery or other forms of catharsis may become all-encompassing needs. Your DCA may seem like a memory. But even a radical life challenge does not mean living without a higher aim.

Below is part of a profile that I wrote of actor Christopher Reeve a year before his 2004 death when he was named *Science of Mind* magazine's "Spiritual Hero of the Year" for 2003. The actor had suffered an equestrian accident in 1995 that rendered him quadriplegic. There are no words for tragedy he suffered. But Reeve demonstrated an extraordinary sense of purpose in pursuing both his own recovery and that of others.

Ambassador of the Miraculous

It would be easy to depict Christopher Reeve as a symbol of hope and determination in the face of an overwhelming disability; as a tireless activist for causes affecting people with disabilities; or as a source of inspiration for others coping with paralysis or disease. The recipient this year of medicine's highest public service honor, The Lasker Award, Reeve measures up to all of these things. But, in actuality, the actor and activist leads a life at once smaller and greater than them all.

In selecting Reeve as the Spiritual Hero of 2003, *Science of Mind* chooses a figure possessed of a unique—though deeply questioning—spiritual life. His life typifies—yet in so many ways differs from—that of millions of Americans who struggle with, or are touched by, severe disability.

As Reeve would be the first to say, he is not a hero of the cinematic variety. "I don't want to sound so noble," he told National Public Radio last year. "There's times when I just get so jealous, I have to admit. You know, I see somebody just get up out of a chair and stretch and I go, 'No, you're not even thinking about what you're doing and how lucky you are to do that.'"

Reeve is not free of the things that make us human. He is, first and foremost, an ordinary person coping with a profound burden: The Superman of the movies was left quadriplegic in a horseback riding accident more than eight years ago. But the dignity, reach, and depth of his struggle make him something much more than ordinary.

Prior to the 1995 equestrian accident that left him paralyzed from the neck down, Reeve was uneasy with questions that touched on life's meaning. Raised as a Presbyterian, he drifted from brief flings with Scientology to rebirthing sessions to motivational workshops, without finding a spiritual perspective with which he felt at home. In recent years, this has changed. "Of necessity I've discovered things within the mind or within the spirit—I don't know exactly where it's located—that never probably would have made themselves known to me without the accident," Reeve said in a radio interview last year. ". . . Oddly enough my mind probably turned against me more before the accident than afterwards."

Today, Reeve holds a set of core beliefs that have emerged in his public statements since the time of his accident. They are:

1. A dogged certainty that the grace of something higher emerges when we muster the will to face our tragedies;
2. the belief that our minds wield a crucial measure of control over the health of our bodies;
3. and the principle that we have the potential to grow beyond what we are told is possible.

When Reeve first suffered his spinal injury, medical authorities believed that spinal tissue could not regrow, severely limiting expectations for recovery. On a five-level rating devised by the American Spinal Injury Association, Reeve was ranked an A—the most severe condition. But as time passed, the unexpected occurred.

In what one neuroscientist called a "miracle," Reeve discovered in 2000 that he could move his left index finger. Moreover, by 2002 Reeve had regained some level of movement over about 20 percent of his body, and physical sensation over nearly 70 percent. "I don't take kindly to ultimatums," he told the Canadian newspaper *The Globe and Mail*. "I think doctors should be very careful before they tell a patient, 'You only have a year to live' or 'You'll never walk again.'"

Reeve and his doctors attribute his success, in part, to a rigorous and dedicated exercise program he has maintained since the accident. There is speculation that Reeve's exercise regimen reestablished some kind of brain-body pathway that was lost when his spine was injured. But Reeve told the English newspaper *The Observer* this year that mental exercise made a powerful impact, too:

> Much of what happens to our bodies is determined by our minds. In 1997, I developed a severe infection on my left ankle due to a shoe being too tight. I was told I'd probably have to have the leg amputated before the whole system was infected. I remember drawing a line in the sand and thinking, 'You can't have my leg, I'm going to need it.' [He tried powerful antibiotics] 'which helped, but after eight days I developed an allergy. I was up at our country house in Northwest Massachusetts, and I remember sitting for hours on the porch staring at the mountains, picturing my ankle the way it used to be and reminding myself that the body wants to heal, to be whole. It took six months, but now you couldn't tell the infection was ever there.

Reeve is as much a pragmatist as an idealist. "I don't believe in false hope. I don't believe in wishful thinking," he told Barbara Walters last year. And he is quick to insist that repairing a spinal cord injury requires far more than positive visualization alone. This has driven Reeve to become a political activist for causes that affect the disabled. He recently thrust himself into the very public debate over embryonic stem cell research.

Like many advocates for the disabled, Reeve believes that embryonic stem-cell research is vital to finding new cures for debilitating diseases, such as paralysis, Lou

Gehrig's Disease, and Alzheimer's Disease. Opponents, however, equate stem cell research, which involves the extraction of stem cells from a fertilized egg, with abortion. Siding with the opponents, President George W. Bush signed an executive order in 2001 banning federal funding for the research.

Reeve has become one of the most outspoken critics of the ban. In his lobbying and in many public forums over the last two years, he has emphasized the promise of stem-cell research, and the irony that the fertilized eggs previously used in such experiments had been castoffs from the many in-vitro fertility clinics in America; they would otherwise have been discarded as biomedical waste. So far, though, Reeve's reasoning has won few converts in the current administration.

Reeve is especially critical of the role that some religious groups played in curtailing stem-cell research. He told the English newspaper *The Guardian* last year:

> We've had a severe violation of the separation of church and state in the handling of what to do about this emerging technology. Imagine if developing a polio vaccine had been a controversial issue. There are religious groups—the Jehovah's Witnesses, I believe—who think it's a sin to have a blood transfusion. What if the president for some reason decided to listen to them, instead of to the Catholics, which is the group he really listens to in making his decisions about embryonic stem-cell research. Where would we be with blood transfusions?

The next day Reeve issued a statement on the website of the Christopher Reeve Paralysis Foundation apologizing to the Catholic Church and to "the faithful of any religion who may have been offended" by his remarks. "However," he insisted, "I do believe in the separation of church and state. Our government should not be influenced by any religion when matters of public policy are being debated."

While Reeve is adamant about the need for research advances, he isn't waiting for new discoveries—he's creating his own possibilities. Reeve is the first to admit that his personal wealth allows him to afford medical care that is far out of reach to most Americans. (He's also been an advocate for insurance reform.) Nonetheless, neuroscientists call Reeve's progress astounding.

When Reeve regained limited movement and a sense of physical sensation, "he did what everybody thought was not possible," Dr. John W. McDonald, director of the spinal cord injury program at Washington University School of Medicine told *The New York Times* last year. "He had the highest level of injury and no recovery for five years. Now he's improving everyday." What makes Reeve's advances all the more remarkable is that they fly in the face of the conventional wisdom that any recovery in a spinal cord injury will occur strictly within the first six months to one year.

What could account for this apparent miracle? Reeve attributes it to a combination of the best that medicine has to offer and to the power of his own thought system and beliefs:

In the seven-plus years since I've been injured, I have never once had a dream in which I'm disabled. I don't know why. I think it's probably because I'm firmly convinced that I am going to walk again. But scientists have been working on a study, and the results will be published at some time, [saying that] if you dream very actively—if you're sailing, if you're running, if you're climbing a mountain or going for a bike ride or whatever—you are firing motor neurons in your brain the same way as if you're actually doing that activity. So perhaps part of my recovery is due to the fact that even while I'm asleep I've been exercising my body.

Whatever the causes, Reeve's case has brought a new sense of determination to many researchers and patients. Years ago, there was simply no progress in many degenerative or paralytic diseases. "Today," Reeve wrote in 2002, "all that has changed. Since the time of my injury, scientists all over the world have been steadily moving forward, although they are not progressing as rapidly as many patients would like. At least they have been saying publicly, and most of us believe privately, that it is no longer appropriate or necessary to use the word 'impossible.' "

The title of his most recent book, *Nothing Is Impossible*, is a motto for all forms of adversity. "When I say nothing's impossible," he told NPR last year, "I don't mean that pigs are gonna fly. But I'm talking about inner resources that we may not know much about, but that we can draw on, and you don't need to nearly die in order to discover these resources. We are capable of so much more than we know. We're just sometimes afraid to venture in that direction."

Earlier this year, Reeve visited Israel—one of the nations that has taken the lead in stem-cell research since the 2001 funding freeze in the United States. He was there to extol the nation's technological advances, and to both seek and spread inspiration. "I saw something very, very extraordinary," he told interviewer Larry King:

> I met a young man who was an Arab-Israeli, and he had been injured for two years, but he underwent surgery within two weeks of his injury, and his injury was just a little worse than mine. He was injured from high up in his chest, then paralyzed all the way down. And two years later—I met him today—he is able to walk with the use of parallel bars, and this is because of the surgery that has been done here in Israel. And it's the most remarkable case of a human recovery that I've ever seen. It moved me tremendously.

Reeve encountered other patients in Israel—including a Druse woman who learned to walk again after a neck fracture—who defied conventional medical expectations. He was visibly moved by what he saw, and the affections ran both ways. "You are my hero," said a 26-year-old man paralyzed from the waist down in a suicide bombing.

In these encounters, and many others, Reeve has, in a way, become an ambassador of the miraculous.

With Reeve's own recovery and the promise that it suggests, his efforts to assist others, and the cases he brings to the world's attention, we find the hero that Christopher Reeve truly is: An embodiment of the voice within each of us saying: never give up.

Working Class Hero

Here is another story—one that I've researched vigorously—of a man who aspired beyond tragedy, and not only found purpose in life but helped countless others to find their purpose, as well.

You've probably heard of the pocket-sized book *As a Man Thinketh*. Written in 1903 by a working-class Englishman named James Allen, *As a Man Thinketh* has found influence all over the world, but nowhere more than in America where it became a founding text of self-help literature. Allen wrote the book nine years before his death from tuberculosis in 1912 at the age of 47—and after a childhood marked by the kind of tragedy that would suggest no way out. But Allen did find a path.

Allen was born in 1864 in the industrial town of Leicester in central England. His father, William, was a successful knitting manufacturer who cultivated James's taste in books and philosophy. A downturn in the textile trade drove William out of business, and in 1879 he traveled to New York City to look for work. His plan was to get settled and pay for the rest of the family to join him. But on the brink of the Christmas season, just after James had turned fifteen, word came back to the Allen household that its patriarch was dead. William had been found robbed and murdered two days after reaching New York. His battered body, its pockets emptied, lay in a city hospital.

James's mother, Martha, a woman who could not read or write, found herself in charge of James and his two younger brothers. "Young Jim" would have to leave school to work as a factory knitter to support the family. The teenager had been his father's favorite. An avid reader, James had spent hours questioning him about life, death, religion, politics, and Shakespeare. "My boy," William told him, "I'll make a scholar of you." Those hopes were gone.

James took up employment locally as a framework knitter, a job that occupied his energies for the next nine years. He sometimes worked fifteen-hour days. But even amid the strains of factory life, he retained the studious bearing that his father had cultivated. When his workmates went out drinking, or caught up on sleep, James studied and read two to three hours a day. Coworkers called him "the Saint" and "the Parson."

James read through his father's collected works of Shakespeare, as well as books of ethics and religion. He grew determined to discover the "central purpose" of life. Around 1889 he found new employment in London as a private secretary and stationer—markedly friendlier vocations to the bookish man than factory work.

By the mid-1890s, James Allen had deepened his inquiry into spiritual philosophies, immersing himself in the works of John Milton, Ralph Waldo Emerson, Walt Whitman, and early translations of the Bhagavad Gita, Tao Te Ching, and the sayings of Buddha. Allen also grew interested in America's New Thought culture through the work of Ralph Waldo Trine, Orison

Swett Marden, and, later, Christian D. Larson. His reading of New Thought literature sharpened his spiritual outlook—in particular his idea that our thoughts are causative and determine our destiny.

After several years of honing his voice writing articles, in 1903 Allen produced his short, immensely powerful meditation, *As a Man Thinketh*. The title came from Proverbs 23:7: *As he thinketh in his heart, so is he.* In Allen's eyes, that brief statement laid out his core philosophy—that a man's thought, if not the cause of his circumstances, is the cause of *himself*, and shapes the tenor of his life.

Toward the end of *As a Man Thinketh*, Allen wrote in a manner that amounted to autobiography:

> Here is a youth hard pressed by poverty and labor; confined long hours in an unhealthy workshop; unschooled, and lacking all the arts of refinement. But he dreams of better things: he thinks of intelligence, of refinement, of grace and beauty. He conceives of, mentally builds up, an ideal condition of life; vision of a wider liberty and a larger scope takes possession of him; unrest urges him to action, and he utilizes all his spare time and means, small though they are, to the development of his latent powers and resources. Very soon so altered has his mind become that the workshop can no longer hold him.

Those lines can be understood as the lesson of James Allen's life: we are as we think, and the mind, focused, educated, and aimed, can lift us to extraordinary and unforeseen heights. That is the "miracle" referred to in the title of this book.

As a Man Thinketh remains one of the most widely read inspirational works in history. It is cited as an influence by figures ranging from Norman Vincent Peale to Michael Jackson. The book's success allowed Allen to dedicate himself to writing for the rest of his life

Allen's wife, Lily, wrote in 1913, a year after her husband's death: "He never wrote *theories*, or for the sake of writing; but he wrote when he had a message, and it became a message *only when he had lived it out in his own life*, and knew that it was good."

Do I Have the *Right* Aim?

Even when not confronted with life-altering circumstances, like Christopher Reeve and James Allen, you may still find yourself facing barriers of the day-to-day variety. You may keep knocking on a door that never seems to open. In such cases, there is a time and a place for asking: Is my aim the right one? As circumstances change—whether geography, technology, your needs, or the public's—it is possible that your DCA may require revision. First, be sure that you understand the nature of what is commonly called failure. As noted, do not mistake temporary setbacks or slow going for failure. If you find yourself stuck in a job that seems impossibly far away from your DCA, it is all the more important to be both clear and certain about your DCA, which is your launching pad away from the old.

That said, it would be dishonest of me not to acknowledge that there are indeed cases where things simply *go wrong*. In such instances your aim may have inadvertently pitted you against indelible barriers or unexpected complications, which necessitate altering your goal or envisioning a new one. *This must be done fearlessly and decisively.* You can begin anew with this book, or any of Napoleon Hill's books. But before you start conceptualizing a new aim, consider what you really want out of your aim. Is it essential that your aim earn your living? I know that is desirable—sometimes achingly so. But is it absolutely necessary?

Let me elucidate what I mean by recalling how a friend set me right about a wrongheaded attitude I developed as an adolescent about art and artists. As a young teenager I wanted to be an actor. I was enrolled at the Long Island High School for the Arts. My teacher, Bert Michaels, was a brilliant, tough-as-nails instructor, as well as an accomplished performer in dramatic, comedic, and musical roles. He played one of the original Jets in the legendary screen version of *West Side Story*, and worked with screen and stage figures including Woody Allen, John Travolta, and Hal Prince. One of my lasting regrets in life is that, as an adolescent, I was not mature enough to take advantage of all that Bert had to offer.

In my junior year in high school my parents got divorced and our family's finances were in a disastrous state. I knew that, very soon, I would need to support myself. I felt that acting was not a financially stable career choice. I opted not to return and instead spent my final year of high school burnishing my grades and getting ready for college—and a career path that I considered more practical.

For many years after college, as I pursued work in publishing, I felt comfortable with my choice to leave acting. I believed that at age fifteen I had made a hard-headed, realistic decision, and I was proud of myself for it. Sometime in my thirties I was telling a friend, a brilliant but struggling stage actor, that I believed that if a person in the dramatic arts reached a certain age and had not broken through, it was time to hang it up and pursue a more practical, financially stable career. If a person wasn't a certain body type, I said, and didn't possess the physical grace necessary for the stage, that, too, meant that he should seek out another vocation.

No, my friend told me, I was wrong. Dedicating yourself to your art as an actor, he said, is a way of life in itself—and a highly worthy one. An artist should never give up because his work by itself doesn't to pay the rent, or doesn't lead to fame or widespread acclaim. An artist is dedicated because of the love for what he's doing, he said, and his commitment to grow in his craft. I was dumbstruck. My friend was entirely right. For all these years I thought that I had been Mr. Practical, Mr. Realistic—but what he was saying possessed a deeper logic.

The fact is, your DCA may never pay the bills. A day job may be a lifelong reality. But, as important as money is, and as important as stability is, there are things that are greater in life. A deep dedication to something that you love, even if it never translates into riding in fancy cars, is an extraordinary gift. It is a purposeful gift. It is *you*. And, as my friend said, serving your vision and your passion can never be the stuff of failure.

My deepest wish for you and everyone reading this book is that you find and pursue your most intimate aim in life. I promise you that on that path, traveled with integrity, craft, and commitment, there is only success.

TAKEAWAY POINTS:

- Even if we do everything right, or think we have, failure is a possibility. But it does not have to be chronic, debilitating, or lifelong.

- Here are four principles to rebound from setbacks: 1) scale your projects so that you can be as self-reliant as possible, at least in the early stages; 2) maintain a higher vision of what you're trying to accomplish; 3) proceed steadily, patiently, and persistently; 4) always ensure that you're performing your tasks with the highest degree of effort and integrity.

- Study Napoleon Hill's eleven traits of personal success. Painstakingly identify which you possess, and which you lack.

- Be certain that you are setting your sights high enough. Make sure that you haven't outgrown your current relationships, venues, and playing field.

- Tragedy is real. But it doesn't preclude a purposeful existence or a renewed aim.

- Economic challenges and pitfalls do not mean you cannot achieve. Study the life of author James Allen.

- Fearlessly consider whether you have the right aim.

- An aim can be right for you even when it doesn't produce fame or wealth.

Closing Note

A Meditation on Fear

I mentioned earlier that procrastination is not only a dream-killer but is a form of fear. Fear is the absolute greatest barrier to your personal progress and capacity for action. As you begin any new undertaking you are likely at one point or another to find yourself gripped by the emotion of fear. Depending on your nature, you may experience this constantly, or at least more often than you would like. I am providing here a condensation of Napoleon Hill's immensely important advice on fear from *Think and Grow Rich*.

Any time that you feel plagued by fear I want you to reflect on this short passage. It is the absolute truth. Let it serve as a beacon to guide you through the storms of fear.

Fear should never be bargained with or capitulated to. It takes the appeal from your personality, destroys the possibility of accurate thinking, diverts concentration of effort, stifles persistence, turns your will power into nothingness, destroys ambition, clouds your memory, and invites failure in every conceivable form.

Fear kills love, assassinates the finer emotions of the heart, discourages friendship, and leads to sleeplessness, misery, and unhappiness.

So pernicious and destructive is the emotion of fear that it is, almost literally, worse than anything that can befall you.

If you suffer from a fear of poverty, reach a decision to get along with whatever wealth you can accumulate WITHOUT WORRY. If you fear the loss of love, reach a decision to get along without love, if that becomes necessary. If you experience a general sense of worry, reach a blanket decision that *nothing that life has to offer is worth the price of fear.* This places Ultimate Truth at your back.

And remember: The greatest of all remedies for fear is a BURNING DESIRE FOR ACHIEVE-MENT, backed by useful action in pursuit of your aim.

Appendix

The Sixteen Laws of Success

There are sixteen laws of success: these traits can be found in life of nearly any exceptional person. Each Napoleon Hill Success Course goes into detail about one or more of these laws. Although it is important to master all sixteen principles, the traits of the whole are, in a sense, inherent in each one, the same way a primeval forest may be traced back to a solitary acorn.

1. A DEFINITE CHIEF AIM. The starting point of all achievement is a definite, passionate, and specific aim. It must be written down, read daily, acted upon constantly, and held in your heart with total commitment.

2. THE MASTER MIND. This is a friendly alliance ranging from as few as two to as many as seven

people who meet at regular intervals to exchange ideas, advice, and sometimes meditations and prayers for one another's success. The Master Mind is critical to your success, as the pooling of intellects results in a sum greater than the parts.

3.   SELF-CONFIDENCE. You must possess or develop the confidence to push on with your plans. If have low self-confidence you can bolster it through meditations, visualizations, autosuggestion, and the Master Mind.

4.   THE HABIT OF SAVING. Thrift is power. You must set aside a definite sum of your earnings in savings. Save at least ten percent of all you earn, and set it aside regularly.

5.   INITIATIVE AND LEADERSHIP. Leadership is essential to success—and initiative is the foundation upon which leadership stands. Initiative means *doing what ought to be done without being told to*. Only those who practice initiative become leaders.

6.   IMAGINATION. In order to have a *definite purpose, self-confidence, initiative* and *leadership*, you must first create these qualities in your *imagination*, and see them as yours. Imagination is the visualizing faculty that lays out your plans and connects knowledge with ideas.

7.   ENTHUSIASM. This is the vital ingredient that allows you to get things done. Without enthusiasm

nothing is possible. With it you demonstrate acts of tireless commitment that sometimes seem miraculous. This is why is your aim must tap your passions. Enthusiasm is the closest thing to a magic elixir.

8.   SELF-CONTROL. Self-control is the force through which your enthusiasm is directed toward constructive ends. Without self-control—of speech, actions, and thought—enthusiasm is like unharnessed lightening: it may strike anywhere. The successful person possesses both *enthusiasm* and *self-control.*

9.   DOING MORE THAN PAID FOR. You are most efficient, and will more quickly and easily succeed, when dedicated to work that you love. When you work with passion, the quality and quantity of your work improve, and you naturally do more and better work than you are paid for. This is why you owe it to yourself to find the work you like best.

10.   PLEASING PERSONALITY. Your personality is the sum total of your characteristics and appearance: the clothes you wear, your facial expressions, the vitality of your body, your handshake, your tone of voice, your thoughts, and most importantly *the character you have developed by those thoughts.*

11.   ACCURATE THOUGHT. Accurate thought is vital to success. Thinking accurately means relying on facts, observations, experience, and data that are

relevant to your aim. This means shunning gossip, rumor, hearsay, idle talk, and casual opinions.

12.   CONCENTRATION. The more you concentrate upon your goal the more you benefit from the law of autosuggestion, through which persistent, emotionally charged ideas impress your subconscious, and organize your thoughts and energies in the service of your definite chief aim. Concentration is a form of power.

13.   COOPERATION. Success cannot be attained singlehandedly. It requires cooperative effort. If your work is based upon cooperation rather than competition, you will get places faster and enjoy an additional reward in happiness. To win the cooperation of others you must offer them a strong motive or reward.

14.   PROFITING BY FAILURE. What we call failure is often temporary defeat. Temporary defeat frequently proves a blessing because it jolts us and redirects our energies along more desirable paths. Reverses, setbacks, and temporary defeat impel the success-drive person toward improved character and plans.

15.   TOLERANCE. Intolerance, bigotry, hostile sarcasm, and bullying make enemies; they disintegrate the organized forces of society; they substitute mob psychology in place of reason. These forces must be mastered before enduring success may be attained.

16. THE GOLDEN RULE. Your thoughts and actions set in motion a power that runs its course in the lives of others, returning, finally, to help or hinder you. This law is immutable—but you can adapt yourself to it and use it as an irresistible force that will carry you to achievement. You do this through living at all times, as best you are able, by the Golden Rule.

Index

About Napoleon Hill

NAPOLEON HILL was born in 1883 in Wise County, Virginia. He worked as a secretary, a reporter for a local newspaper, the manager of a coalmine and a lumberyard, and attended law school, before taking a job as a journalist for *Bob Taylor's Magazine*, an inspirational and general-interest journal. In 1908, Hill interviewed steel magnate Andrew Carnegie who told him that success could be distilled into a set of practical principles. The industrialist urged Hill to interview high achievers in every field to discover these principles. Hill dedicated himself to this study for more than twenty years, and distilled what he found into *The Law of Success* (1928), *Think and Grow Rich* (1937), and his other classic works. Hill spent the rest of his life documenting and refining the principles of success. After a career as an author, publisher, lecturer, and business consultant, the motivational pioneer died in 1970 in South Carolina. Learn more about Napoleon Hill and the Napoleon Hill Foundation at www.NapHill.org.

About Mitch Horowitz

MITCH HOROWITZ is a writer and publisher with a lifelong interest in man's search for meaning. The PEN Award-winning author of *Occult America* and *One Simple Idea: How the Lessons of Positive Thinking Can Transform Your Life*, Mitch has written on everything from the war on witches to the secret life of Ronald Reagan for *The New York Times*, *The Wall Street Journal*, *Salon*, and Time.com. *The Washington Post* says Mitch "treats esoteric ideas and movements with an even-handed intellectual studiousness that is too often lost in today's raised-voice discussions." *Paris Match* writes "Mitch Horowitz, a specialist in American esotericism, traces the history of positive thinking and its influence . . . takes us far from naive doctrines." Mitch narrates popular audio books including *Alcoholics Anonymous* and Gildan Media's Condensed Classics Library. He is a monthly columnist for *Science of Mind* magazine. Visit him at www.MitchHorowitz .com and @MitchHorowitz.

Also by Mitch Horowitz

*One Simple Idea: How Positive Thinking
Reshaped Modern Life*

*Occult America: The Secret History of
How Mysticism Shaped Our Nation*

*Mind As Builder: The Positive-Mind
Metaphysics of Edgar Cayce**

*The Power of the Master Mind
(The Napoleon Hill Success Course Series)**

*Awakened Mind: How Thoughts Become
Reality (The Master Class Series)**

*Miracle: The Ideas of Neville Goddard
(The Master Class Series)**

*available in Gildan Audio editions

Coming Soon...

From acclaimed historian and New Thought author

Mitch Horowitz

Available February 2018, from Gildan Press

Also look for the Condensed Classics Library.
Each abridged, narrated, and introduced
by Mitch Horowitz.
Available in audio, print, and digital.

How to Attract Good Luck

Alcoholics Anonymous

The Secret Door to Success

The Magic of Believing

The Science of Getting Rich

Your Faith Is Your Fortune

A Message to Garcia

Acres of Diamonds

The Law of Success

The Secret of the Ages

Think and Grow Rich

The Power of Your Subconscious Mind

Public Speaking to Win

The Game of Life And How to Play it

Notes

Notes

Notes

Notes